ESSENTIAL
TENERIFE

Original text by Andrew Sanger
Updated by Barbara and Stillman Rogers

© AA Media Limited 2009
First published 2007
Revised 2009

ISBN: 978-0-7495-6130-7

Published by AA Publishing, a trading name of AA Media Limited, whose registered office is Fanum House, Basing View, Basingstoke, Hampshire RG21 4EA. Registered number 06112600.

AA Media Limited retains the copyright in the original edition © 2000 and in all subsequent editions, reprints and amendments

Colour separation: MRM Graphics Ltd
Printed and bound in Italy by Printer Trento S.r.l.

A03804
Maps in this title produced from mapping:
© KOMPASS GmbH, A-6063 Rum, Innsbruck

The essence of...

Contents

About this book

This book is divided into five sections.

The essence of Tenerife pages 6–19
Introduction; Features; Food and drink; Short break including the 10 Essentials

Planning pages 20–33
Before you go; Getting there; Getting around; Being there

Best places to see pages 34–55
The unmissable highlights of any visit to Tenerife

Best things to do pages 56–81
Top beaches; places to have lunch; best festivals; top activities; places to take the children; boat trips and more

Exploring pages 82–186
The best places to visit in Tenerife, organized by area

Maps

All map references are to the maps on the covers. For example, La Laguna has the reference ✚ 9B – indicating the grid square in which it is to be found

Admission prices

Inexpensive (under €3)
Moderate (€3–€6)
Expensive (over €6)

Hotel prices

Prices are per room per night:
€ budget (under €65)
€€ moderate (€65–€90)
€€€ expensive to luxury (over €90)

Restaurant prices

Price for a three-course meal per person without drinks:
€ budget (under €15)
€€ moderate (€15–€30)
€€€ expensive (over €30)

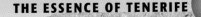

Tenerife is like two places in one. In the north it's
Spanish and lived-in, with working towns and villages
amid a landscape of almost tropical, productive
lushness. In the south it's a dry (almost rain-free)
holiday land of vibrant entertainment, resorts and
hotels, devoted to giving millions of visitors a good
time. This combination appeals equally to those who
revel in days in the sun and nights on the town and
those who delight in the 'real' Tenerife, with its
beautiful volcanic landscape and its friendly people.

features

A layer of tourism clings to the surface of Tenerife, where 4 million tourists a year outnumber the island population of 800,000. It's a prosperous tradition that dates back to the mid-19th century, and it's not all bad – most visitors stay in sun-baked southern parts of the island where locals have rarely lived, leaving inland parts peaceful and unspoiled. The challenge for visitors is to get beneath the surface, peel back the layer of tourism and discover that Tenerife is not just a holiday isle.

HISTORY
● The island is also a relic of colonial Spain, with reminders of the *conquistadores* and of Spain's enterprise, power and wealth centuries ago. The Canaries feel close to the former colonies in Latin America, where so many Tinerfeños went to live. Holidays and history aside, there's also the Tenerife of today in the villages, the hills and the backstreets of Santa Cruz and La Laguna. Here are the real bars and *restaurantes*, the plazas, the sounds and the people of Spain.

THE ORIGINAL ISLANDERS
● Peel back the colonial and modern-day patina, and there's yet another level – out there beyond the

towns and villages. The Guanches, the native islanders, are long gone, but take a walk alone in the balmy, luxuriant hills, or in the desolate Cañadas and you'll sense the air of mystery that they bequeathed. There are several important relics of Guanche culture on the island, notably the remarkable groups of ceremonial step-pyramid platforms at Güímar. Through them, it is evident that Tenerife belongs neither to the tourists nor to the Spanish, but to the Atlantic, to Africa and to the snow-capped volcano that gave the island its Guanche name.

GEOGRAPHY

● Though Spanish, Tenerife is closer to the Sahara – only 300km (186 miles) or so from the coast of Africa – and some 1,500km (930 miles) from Spain. It lies in the western half of the Canary Islands archipelago, and is the largest island in the group, 130km (80 miles) across at its widest point, and 90km (56 miles) from north to south. La Gomera, the second smallest of the Canary Islands, just 23 by 25km (14 by 15.5 miles), lies 32km (20 miles) from Tenerife's southwestern shore.

CLIMATE

● The climate is close to perfect: in the mostly dry south temperatures average 19°C (66°F) in winter and about 25°C in (77°F) summer (ideal for visitors), while the prevailing trade winds bring moist air or rain to the north (good for agriculture and wild plant life). Beautiful scenery, from fine sand beaches to the pine-clad foothills and moonscapes of volcanic El Teide, makes this a fascinating place to explore.

food & drink

With so many popular eating places in the resorts focusing on holiday favourites like pizza, pasta and paella, it's easy to forget that most inland restaurants offer traditional local cuisine, usually in cool, simple, tiled surroundings. Look out for the word *tipico*, meaning roughly 'traditional' or 'local'.

FISH AND VEGETABLES

Tenerife's staple is quality fresh fish. Most popular are *vieja* (parrot fish or sun fish) and *merluza* (hake), *abade*, *mero* and *cabrilla* (all forms of sea bass) and *cherne* (a larger bass often cut and served in steaks). Fish is usually prepared in a plain and simple way, such as grilled or fried, and served with a dressing of oil, vinegar and mildly hot peppers or *mojo* (► 15), together with a vegetable or two. Salted fish is also traditional. Among the vegetables, the most typical are *papas arrugadas*, or wrinkly potatoes. These delectable salty new potatoes, cooked in their skins with plenty of salt until the water has completely boiled away, are properly served with *mojo*. They are a must for anyone not on a low-sodium diet, and on their own make a delicious snack.

STEWS

The people of Tenerife are fond of hearty stews, usually combining several meats, including pork and rabbit, with chickpeas and vegetables and often thickened with *gofio* (see below). *Rancho canario* and *puchero* are traditional stews. *Potaje*, vegetable stew, is a less meaty alternative (though vegetarians beware, even this might contain a little meat!). The fishy version is *sancocho*, a thick stew of salted fish and vegetables. Served with bread, such stews can make a complete meal.

GOFIO

Nothing is more Canarian than *gofio*, the versatile staple of the native Guanche diet that is still very much in use. A rough roasted wholemeal flour (usually of maize, but possibly also of barley, wheat or even chickpeas), it appears in soups, as a sort of polenta, as a paste mixed with vegetables, or as breads, cakes and puddings.

MOJO

One of the most genuinely Canarian words on the menu is *mojo*. Meat, fish, cheese and vegetables may all be served *con mojo* (with *mojo*), a piquant sauce of varying degrees of spiciness depending on what it accompanies. The two main types are *mojo verde* (green), its parsley and coriander recipe giving a cool, sharp flavour, and *mojo rojo*, the spicier, red sauce made with chillies and peppers.

DESSERTS

Banana flambé is a must in the resorts, but is not as common in authentic local restaurants. *Gofio* is used to make desserts such as the semolina-like *flan gofio*, or popular *frangollo*, which is made of *gofio* and dried fruit. Syrupy, nutty *bienmesabe* pudding is the Canarians' favourite.

WINE

Tenerife's wines have been enjoyed in Europe for centuries, traditionally a sweet, rich, heady brew, made from the *malvasia* grape used in the old-fashioned malmsey. Nowadays Tenerife's excellent wines can be dry or sweet, red or white. The main wine-growing area is around El Sauzal, just north of Puerto de la Cruz. La Gomera, too, makes drinkable table wine. Make sure you try the sweet dessert wine of Vallehermoso.

Short break

If you only have a short time in Tenerife, and would like to take home some unforgettable memories, you can venture beyond the tourist hotspots and capture a real flavour of the island. The following suggestions will give you a good variety of experiences and places to see that will make your visit very special. Even if you only have time for one or two of these, you will find the heart and soul of the island.

● **Go up El Teide** The high point of Tenerife is a snow-capped dormant volcano (➤ 40–41), which was worshipped by the original inhabitants of the island. The climb to the top is a rewarding experience for fit, experienced hikers, but the spectacular panoramic views can be enjoyed less strenuously by taking the cable car to a point just short of the summit. From up here you can see almost the whole of the Canary Islands.

● **Experience Playa de las Américas** This package holiday dreamland may be far removed from the reality of home, but it is undeniably an established part of island life. You can't get the full picture of Tenerife without seeing a little of what

THE ESSENCE OF TENERIFE

goes on in its foremost purpose-built resort, with its artificial beaches, all-night discos and English-style pubs and restaurants (➤ 155).

- **Go bananas** Bananas are an important crop on Tenerife, so be sure to enjoy them whenever you get the opportunity. Have them flambéed for dessert, sip banana liqueur, buy some souvenirs made out of banana leaves and visit Bananera El Guanche (➤ 120–121).

- **Eat a Canarian stew** There's no better way to get the flavour (literally) of a place than to try what the locals eat. Try *potaje, rancho canario* or *puchero* – vegetables and meat simmered to a savoury perfection.

- **Try local flavours** The flavourful local sauce, *mojo,* is a delicacy that must be tried. Served with fish or *papas arrugadas* (wrinkly potatoes), it's likely to be the most Canarian thing on the menu.

- **Drink a local wine** Long before any tourist set foot on the island, the development of wines to rival those on mainland Spain was one of the first big successes for colonial Tenerife. The island's wines have remained important ever since, and little La Gomera has good local wines too.

- **Get out of the resorts** Having experienced what draws most of Tenerife's 4 million visitors each year, the next thing to do is explore the rest of

the island. Whether you walk, rent a car or bicycle, get away from the southern resorts to experience the Tenerife most tourists never see.

● **Watch a whale** Whales and dolphins live just off southern Tenerife and La Gomera, and you can get up close to them on one of the boat excursions. It's an unforgettable experience.

● **Have fun at a fiesta** It's an unusual week in the Tenerife calendar that doesn't have at least one fiesta, and you can join in the fun alongside the locals. Ask the tourist office what's on next.

● **Go to another island** Take the ferry to La Gomera to discover a truly unspoiled Canary Island. If you're based on La Gomera, take the boat trip over to Tenerife, if only to visit El Teide.

Planning

Before you go

WHEN TO GO

JAN	FEB	MAR	APR	MAY	JUN	JUL	AUG	SEP	OCT	NOV	DEC
20°C	21°C	23°C	24°C	25°C	27°C	28°C	29°C	28°C	26°C	23°C	20°C
68°F	70°F	73°F	75°F	77°F	81°F	82°F	84°F	82°F	79°F	73°F	68°F

🌤 High season   🌤 Low season

Temperatures are the average daily maximum for each month. Tenerife is famous as a year-round destination and though there can be winter cloud and some rain in the north, the main holiday areas in the south are almost rain-free all year round. The upper reaches of the peak of Mount Teide are generally snow-capped in winter and well into spring.

The island is strongly influenced by the prevailing trade winds, and it can be windy at any time of year, particularly on the northwest coast, but it's usually a warm wind. The peak holiday season is inevitably in the summer, but the climate is pleasant all year round. A good time to come, however, is in spring when the air is crisp and the flowers are in bloom.

WHAT YOU NEED

		UK	Germany	USA	Netherlands	Spain
●	Required					
○	Suggested					
▲	Not required					

Some countries require a passport to remain valid for a minimum period (usually at least six months) beyond the date of entry – check before you travel.

	UK	Germany	USA	Netherlands	Spain
Passport (or National Identity Card where applicable)	●	●	●	●	●
Visa (regulations can change – check before you travel)	▲	▲	▲	▲	▲
Onward or Return Ticket	▲	▲	○	▲	▲
Health Inoculations (tetanus and polio)	▲	▲	▲	▲	▲
Health Documentation (► 23, Health Insurance)	▲	▲	▲	▲	▲
Travel Insurance	○	○	○	○	○
Driving Licence (national)	●	●	●	●	●
Car Insurance Certificate	●	●	●	●	●
Car Registration Document	●	●	●	●	●

WEBSITES

Spanish National Tourist Office
www.tourspain.co.uk
www.spain.info
Local information
www.puntoinfo.idecnet.com
www.canaries-live.com
www.discover-tenerife.co.uk
www.gomera-island.com

UK Passport Service
www.ukpa.gov.uk
Health advice for travellers
www.dh.gov.uk
Flights and information
www.cheapflights.co.uk
www.thisistravel.co.uk
www.flymonarch.com

TOURIST OFFICES AT HOME

In the UK Spanish National Tourist Office, 2nd Floor 79 New Cavendish Street, London W1W 6XB ☎ 020 7486 8077; www.spain.info

In the USA Tourist Office of Spain, 666 Fifth Avenue, 35th floor New York, NY 10103 ☎ 212 265-8822; www.okspain.org Also in Chicago, LA and Miami.

HEALTH INSURANCE

It is essential to have good health cover for medical emergencies. EU citizens with a European Health Insurance Card (EHIC) can receive health care in Tenerife under the state scheme. Details can be found at www.dh.gov.uk. To claim on health insurance you may need to show that you did request treatment under the state health service with an EHIC.

Emergency dental treatment is covered by most medical insurance (but not with an EHIC). Hotels and holiday reps can advise on a local dentist.

TIME DIFFERENCES

| GMT Noon | Tenerife Noon | Spain 1PM | USA (NY) 7AM | USA (West Coast) 4AM | New Zealand Midnight |

The time in Tenerife (and all Canary Islands) is the same as in the UK. The islands change to Summer Time (GMT+1) on the same date as the UK and the rest of the EU. The Canaries are therefore one hour behind mainland Spain, and 5 hours ahead of the Eastern US.

NATIONAL HOLIDAYS

1 January *Año Nuevo* (New Year's Day)

6 January *Los Reyes* (Epiphany)

2 February *La Candelaria* (Candlemas)

19 March *San José* (St Joseph's Day)

March/April *Pascua* (Easter) Thu, Fri, Sun of Easter Week, and following Mon

1 May *Día del Trabajo* (Labour Day)

30 May *Día de las Islas Canarias* (Canary Islands Day)

May/June *Corpus Christi*

25 July *Santiago* (St James' Day)

15 August *Asunción* (Assumption)

12 October *Hispanidad* (Columbus Day)

1 November *Todos los Santos* (All Saints' Day)

6 December *Constitución* (Constitution Day)

8 December *Immaculada Concepción* (Immaculate Conception)

25 December *Navidad* (Christmas)

Banks, businesses, museums and most shops are closed on these days.

WHAT'S ON WHEN

January *Cabalgata de los Reyes Magos* (The Three Kings Cavalcade, 5–6 Jan): many places, especially Santa Cruz and Valle Gran Rey (La Gomera).
Fiestas (17–22 Jan): Garachico, Icod de los Vinos, Los Realejos and San Sebastián (La Gomera).

February *Carnaval:* festivities climax on Shrove Tuesday. Main focus is Santa Cruz; parades in other towns including Puerto de la Cruz (► 64–65).
Candelaria (Candlemas, 2 Feb): big festival and pilgrimage in many places, especially Candelaria.
Carnaval (end Feb): Los Cristianos – marks the end of Carnival Month.
Carnaval (end Feb/early Mar): San Sebastián (La Gomera).

March/April *San José holiday* (19 Mar). *Semana Santa* (Holy Week):

big events, often sober, all over the islands during Easter Week.
Fiestas (25 Apr): notably at Icod de los Vinos, Teguesta and Agulo
(La Gomera).

May/June *Día de las Islas Canarias* (Canary Islands Day, 30 May): all over.
Corpus Christi (late May/early Jun): Octavo (8 days) celebrations across
the island, especially La Orotava, La Laguna and Vilaflor. Streets adorned
with sand-and-flower designs.
Romería (after Corpus Christi): the season of local pilgrimages.
Fiesta de San Juan (24 Jun): midsummer celebrations, notably at
Vallehermoso (La Gomera).

July *Fiestas del Gran Poder* (15 Jul): Puerto de la Cruz – processions,
parades, fireworks and fun.
Santiago (25 Jul): festive public holiday; Santa Cruz, celebration of the
defeat of Nelson in 1797.

August *Asunción and Nuestra Señora de la Candelaria* (14–15 Aug):
Candelaria – important island-wide pilgrimage.
Romería de San Roque (16 Aug): Garachico – colourful local event.
Nuestra Señora del Carmen (30 Aug): Los Cristianos – popular,
lively fiesta.

September *Semana Colombina* (Columbus Week, 1–6 Sep): San
Sebastián (La Gomera).
Virgen de Buen Paso (15 Sep): Alajeró (La Gomera).
Fiestas (mid-Sep): La Laguna and Tacoronte.

October *Día de la Hispanidad* (12 Oct): celebrating Columbus.
Fiesta de los Cacharros (Pots and Pans, 29 Oct): noisy fiesta to celebrate
the new wine.

December *New Year's Eve* (31 Dec): as the clock strikes midnight, at
every chime eat a grape and spit out the seeds. If you find this easy, also
take a sip of *cava* at every chime.

Getting there

BY AIR

Reina Sofía Airport to:

Puerto de la Cruz: 100km (62 miles)   🚗 2 hours

Playa de las Américas: 15km (9 miles)   🚗 25 minutes

Almost all flights to Tenerife arrive at Reina Sofía (or Tenerife Sur) Airport (tel: 922 759200), on the Costa del Silencio, just east of Playa de las Américas in the south. The airport tourist information booth (tel: 922 392037) in the arrivals hall, open Mon–Fri 9–9, Sat 9–1, has general information, including a handy map. Staff can help with accommodation and public transport, and will point the way to buses, taxis and car-rental outlets in the airport. The distance from the airport to Puerto de la Cruz is 100km (62 miles), with a journey time of 2 hours. To Playa de las Américas it's 15km (9 miles), with a journey time of 25 minutes.

You can pick up public buses of TITSA (Transportes Interurbanos de Tenerife SA, tel: 922 531300; www.titsa.com) to several destinations. Number 487 goes to Playa de las Américas via Los Cristianos. They run hourly from about 8am to 10pm and take 50–65 minutes. Bus No 341 connects to Santa Cruz de Tenerife. Departures are roughly hourly from 6:50am and the journey takes about 90 minutes on the *autopista*. Bus No 340 to Puerto de la Cruz leaves only four times a day and takes anything up to two and a half hours.

Taxi fares are reasonable to Los Cristianos or Playa de las Américas, but expensive to Santa Cruz de Tenerife or Puerto de la Cruz.

A second, smaller airport, Los Rodeos or Tenerife Norte (tel: 922 635974), at La Laguna in the north of the island, is used mainly for inter-island flights (including a daily service to La Gomera with Binter Canarias, tel: 902 391392; www.binternet.com) and flights to and from mainland Spain. It is 10km (6 miles) west of Santa Cruz de Tenerife and 26km (16 miles) east of Puerto de la Cruz. A complete overhaul has given it a sparkling modern terminal.

TITSA bus No 107 runs between the airport and the centre of Santa Cruz de Tenerife every hour or so, terminating at the Estación de Guaguas, the main bus station. The trip takes about 30 minutes. Bus No 108 to Icod de los Vinos runs via La Orotava and takes an hour. Bus No 102 is a little slower and goes via La Laguna, 3km (2 miles) from Tenerife Norte Airport. From the airport it continues west to Buenavista. You can get a taxi to any northeast destination at a reasonable cost. Trips to Santa Cruz de Tenerife take 20 minutes, to Puerto de la Cruz 30 minutes.

BY SEA

Independent travellers can reach the islands by boat from Cadiz, on the Spanish mainland, a journey of around two days. Inter-island ferries and hydrofoils connect Tenerife and La Gomera to the other islands.

In Santa Cruz, Estación Marítima, the city's main ferry port, is at the northeast end of town. Spain's national ferry company, Trasmediterránea (tel: 902 454645; www.trasmediterranea.co.uk) has a service from Cádiz (once a week) and jetfoils from Las Palmas on Gran Canaria (three a day), plus daily services (except Sun) from Morro Jable on Fuerteventura. A weekly ferry arrives from Santa Cruz de la Palma on La Palma. It's a 10-minute walk to the centre of town from the main terminal, the Muelle de Ribera, or take a taxi. Other companies operate from quays a little closer to the centre. Tickets are available at most travel agents or from ferry companies' booths in the Muelle de Ribera building on Avenida Anaga.

In Los Cristianos, Estación Marítima is the main arrival/departure point for La Gomera, plus La Palma and El Hierro (once or twice daily). The terminal is a short walk from the centre. A short bus or taxi ride takes you further around the coast to Playa de las Américas.

At La Gomera, Fred Olsen (tel: 902 100107; www.fredolsen.es), runs up to five jetfoils (40 mins), and one car ferry (80 mins) a day to Los Cristianos. Garajonay Expres (tel: 902 343450; www.garajonayexpres.com) has three fast ferries a day from Los Cristianos to San Sebastián.

Getting around

PUBLIC TRANSPORT
Buses The local name for buses is *guaguas* (pronounced wah-wahs). Stops are called *paradas* and indicated by the letter 'P'. A bus station is an *estación de guaguas*. Most Tenerife buses are operated by TITSA. Services are fairly frequent and inexpensive on main routes; in remote areas, and throughout La Gomera, service is intermittent and generally of little use to visitors.

Fares are quite reasonable (less than €2 between Tenerife Sur airport and Los Cristianos, for example). The *Bonobus* card is good value if you plan to use the bus a lot. It entitles you to a 30 per cent discount on fares and also offers discounted admission at some museums.

Main bus stations:
- Avenida Béthencourt, Playa de las Américas ☎ 922 795427
- Avenida 3 Mayo 47, Santa Cruz ☎ 922 218122
- Calle de Cupido, Puerto de la Cruz ☎ 922 381807
- La Laguna ☎ 922 259412

Many of the main attractions operate free shuttle buses to and from the resorts.

INTER-ISLAND FERRIES
There are several ferry services linking the islands, and there's also a service to mainland Spain.
- Transmediterránea (Estación. Marítima, Muelle de Ribera, Santa Cruz ☎ 922 842244) operate ferries to mainland Spain and to the other Canary Islands from the port in Santa Cruz.
- From Los Cristianos (Muelle de Los Cristianos) to La Gomera (Estacíon Marítima, Puerto de San Sebastían de la Gomera ☎ 922 871324).
- Estación Jet-Foil (Muelle Norte, Santa Cruz ☎ 922 243012): 80-minute jetfoil to Las Palmas de Gran Canaria.

- Estación Hidro-Foil (Los Cristianos harbour ☎ 922 796178; 902 343450): hydrofoils to La Gomera (35 mins).
- Ferry Gomera (Los Cristianos harbour ☎ 922 790215): to La Gomera (90 mins).
- Fred Olsen (Muelle Ribera, Santa Cruz ☎ 922 628200): to La Gomera and Gran Canaria from Los Cristianos and Santa Cruz.

TAXIS

Taxis display an SP licence plate *(servicio público)*. Some taxi ranks display fares between principal destinations. In addition, taxi drivers offer island tours for up to four passengers; negotiate the fare before you set off.

CAR RENTAL

It is relatively inexpensive to rent a car on Tenerife, but will cost more on La Gomera; be sure to book ahead. Major international car rental companies have desks at the airport. There are some reputable and efficient local firms, too, which might give you a good deal, but get recommendations – and make sure you get an after-hours emergency number. The rental companies should provide insurance cover for the vehicle and driver. The minimum age for renting a car is 21.

DRIVING

- Drive on the right.
- Speed limit on motorways: 100–120kph (62–74mph)
  Speed limit on other main roads: 100kph (62mph)
  Speed limit in towns: 40kph (25mph)
- Seat belts are compulsory for all passengers, with instantaneous fines for non-compliance. Children under 10, except babies in rear-facing baby seats, are not allowed to ride in front seats.
- Driving under the influence of alcohol is strictly illegal and random breath tests are carried out.
- On-the-spot fines are levied for not stopping at a Stop sign or overtaking where forbidden.
- Unleaded petrol *(sin plomo)* is the norm.
- Petrol stations on main roads are usually open 24 hours and most take credit cards. Off main roads they may be far apart, closed on Sunday, and don't always take credit cards.

Being there

TOURIST OFFICES

Tenerife
Airport Tenerife Sur Reina Sofía
☎ 922 392037.
Garachico ✉ Calle Estéban de
Ponte 5 ☎ 922 133461.
Los Cristianos ✉ Casa de la
Cultura, Plaza del Pescador
☎ 922 757137.
Playa de las Américas ✉ Avenida
Rafael Puig 19 ☎ 922 797668.
Puerto de la Cruz ✉ Plaza de

Europa 5 ☎ 922 386000.
Santa Cruz ✉ Palacio Insular
(ground floor), Plaza de España
☎ 922 239592.

La Gomera
Playa de Santiago ✉ Edificio Las
Vistas, Local 8, Avenida Marítima
☎ 922 895650.
San Sebastián ✉ Calle Real 4
☎ 922 141512.

MONEY
The euro (€) is the single currency of the
European Monetary Union, which has to
date been adopted by 16 of the member
states, including Spain. Banknotes are
issued in denominations of 5, 10, 20, 50,
100, 200 and 500 euros; coins in 1, 2, 5, 10,
20 and 50 cents, and 1 and 2 euros. ATMs
(cash machines) can be found in all towns on
Tenerife. Euro travellers' cheques are widely
accepted throughout the island.

TIPS/GRATUITIES

Yes ✓ No ✕		
Hotels and restaurants	✕	included
Room service	✓	€1–2
Cafés/bars	✓	change
Taxis	✓	10%
Porters	✓	€1–2
Chambermaids	✓	€1–2
Cloakroom/washroom attendants	✓	50c
Tour guides	✓	€2–3

POSTAL AND INTERNET SERVICES

Postboxes are yellow and often have a slot marked *Extranjeros* for mail to foreign countries. Letters and postcards to the UK cost 53c (up to 20g). Air letters and postcards to the US/Canada cost 78c (up to 15g), and letters within Spain cost 82c. Buy stamps at tobacconists, souvenir shops or post offices *(correos y telegrafos)*.

Tourist offices have lists of local internet points, which can be found in most towns of any size. Many hotels have internet for guests' use, but few except those in the higher range have in-room service. Cost varies widely, so if the first place you try seems too pricey, try elsewhere.

TELEPHONES

For the Spanish operator, dial 1009. For the EU international operator, dial 1008. To use a phone in a bar, pay the barman at the end of the call – he has a meter to check the cost. To use a public pay phone, you'll usually need *una tarjeta de telefóno* (phone card) available from tobacconists. There are also phone offices *(telefónica internacional)* where you pay a clerk after the call.

Emergency telephone numbers
Police 091
General Emergencies 112
Ambulance 061

International dialling codes
First dial 00, wait for a change of tone, then dial the country code, for example:
UK 44
Ireland 353
USA 1
Spain Dial number only

EMBASSIES AND CONSULATES

UK Santa Cruz
☎ 922 286863
USA Madrid
☎ 91 5872200

Germany Santa Cruz
☎ 922 248820
Canada Madrid
☎ 91 4233250

ELECTRICITY
The voltage is 220–225 volts. Sockets take the standard European two-round-pin plugs. You will need to bring an adaptor for any British or North American appliances with their usual plugs, and visitors from North America should change the voltage setting on appliances, or bring a voltage transformer.

HEALTH AND SAFETY
Sun advice Use generous amounts of sun cream with a high protection factor. A wide-brimmed hat and a T-shirt (even when swimming) are advisable for children.
Medication Over-the-counter proprietary brands of analgesics and popular remedies are available at all pharmacies. All medicines must be paid for, even if prescribed by a doctor.
Safe water Tap water is safe all over the islands, except where signs indicate otherwise. Bottled water is recommended.

OPENING HOURS

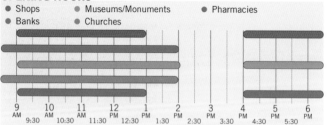

- Shops
- Banks
- Museums/Monuments
- Churches
- Pharmacies

Most shops are open Mon–Sat 9–1, 4–8. Pharmacies are the same but closed on Sat afternoons. Normally at least one is open after hours (the rota is displayed on pharmacy doors). Banks and post offices are open Mon–Fri 8:30–2 and Sat 9–1 (although banks close one hour earlier on Sat between 1 Jun and 31 Oct). Museums are open 4–7pm with larger sites open mornings too.

LANGUAGE

It is helpful to know some basic Spanish. Pronunciation guide: *b* almost like a *v*; *c* before *e* or *i* sounds like *th* otherwise like *k*; *d* like English *d* or *th*; *g* before *e* or *i* is a guttural *h*, between vowels like *h*, otherwise like *g*; *h* always silent; *j* guttural *h*; *ll* like English *lli* (as in 'million'); *ñ* sounds like *ni* in 'onion'; *qu* sound like *k*; *v* sounds a little like *b*; *z* like English *th*.

yes/no	*sí/no*	I don't speak	*No hablo*
please/thank you	*por favor/gracias*	Spanish	*español*
hello/hi/good day	*hola/buenos días*	I am .../I have ..	*Soy .../Tengo ...*
sorry, pardon me	*perdón*	help!	*!socorro!*
bye, see you	*hasta luego*	how much?	*¿cuánto es?*
that's fine	*está bien*	open/closed	*abierto/cerrado*
what?	*¿como?*	the toilet	*los servicios*
hotel	*hotel*	reservation	*una reserva*
room	*una habitación*	rate	*la tarifa*
single/double/	*individual/doble/*	breakfast	*el desayuno*
twin	*con dos camas*	bathroom	*el cuarto de baño*
one/two nights	*una noche/dos*	shower	*la ducha*
	noches	key	*la llave*
bureau de change	*cambio*	pounds sterling	*la libra esterlina*
post office	*correo*	banknote	*un billete de banco*
cash machine/ATM	*cajero automático*	travellers' cheques	*cheques de viaje*
foreign exchange	*cambio (de divisas)*	credit card	*tarjeta de crédito*
restaurant/café-bar	*restaurante/bar*	dessert	*el postre*
table/menu	*una mesa/la carta*	water/beer	*agua/cerveza*
today's set menu	*el plato del día*	(house) wine	*vino (de la casa)*
wine list	*la carta de vinos*	bill	*la cuenta*
plane	*el avión*	ticket	*un billete*
airport	*el aeropuerto*	single/return...	*de ida / ...de ida y*
bus	*el autobús*		*vuelta*
	('guagua')	timetable	*el horario*
ferry/terminal	*el ferry/terminus*	seat	*un asiento*

Best places to see

Casa de los Balcones, La Orotava

The most famous sight in the sedate Spanish colonial hilltown of La Orotava is a rambling 17th-century mansion.

Pretty potted geraniums decorate the balconies looking over Calle San Francisco, but it's not these that give the house its name: enter the impressive front doors and you will find the exquisitely carved wooden balconies of the courtyard. Here abundant refreshing greenery, earthenware pots and an old wine press give a cool, elegant air. The building's history is told in the museum upstairs: originally it consisted of two separate houses built in 1632 as homes for prosperous colonists.

Downstairs, the busy souvenir and craft shop has the additional attraction of local craftspeople demonstrating how to roll a cigar, weave a basket, or paint sand in readiness for the big Corpus Christi celebrations. This unusual shop sells a wide range of high-quality handcrafted items such as Spanish and Canarian lace and linen, and traditional embroidery. Small items offer the opportunity to buy good quality, local goods at affordable prices.

Some embroidery is made on the premises, as the Casa de los Balcones also serves as a highly regarded school for training small numbers of pupils in the traditional methods and designs of Canarian embroidery, which would probably have disappeared altogether if not for its efforts.

✠ 7D ✉ Calle San Francisco 3, La Orotava ☎ 922 330629
🕐 Mon–Sat 8:30–6:30 ✋ Museum: inexpensive; courtyard

and craft shop: free  Restaurants and bars in Plaza de la
Constitución 🚌 TITSA buses 101, 107, 108 from Santa Cruz;
345, 348, 350, 352 from Puerto de la Cruz every half hour

2 Drago Milenario

The *drago* or dragon tree is a species peculiar to the Canary Islands, and this amazing, ancient example has become an island emblem.

Just how old is this extraordinary tree? The age of the 'Thousand-Year-Old Dragon Tree' is often exaggerated to two or even three thousand years.

In reality, this majestic specimen, the oldest known, probably dates back about 600 years.

More remarkable perhaps is that the species – *Dracaena draco*, closely related to the yucca – has barely evolved since the age of the dinosaurs. It has long been an object of fascination to botanists and naturalists, and to those sensitive to magic and mystery. That's partly because of its curious form, growing like a bundle of separate trunks clinging together before bursting to create the *drago's* distinctive mushroom shape. Weirdest of all is the *drago's* strange resin, which turns as red as blood on contact with the air. Though nothing is known of Guanche beliefs, many people insist that the *drago* was worshipped by these first inhabitants of the island, who used its resin for embalming.

Standing 17m (56ft) high and with a diameter of 6m (20ft), the Drago Milenario is the main attraction at Icod de los Vinos, an attractive little west-coast wine town that was the site of Tenerife's largest Guanche settlements when the Europeans arrived. The Drago Milenario was already mature when the Spanish took control. It is now protected in a small botanic garden, but can be clearly seen from the adjacent plaza. Bars and souvenir shops here cash in on the tree's mystique. Different from the rest, and an attraction in itself, is the pretty, traditional shop, Casa del Drago.

✚ 4D 🖂 Parque del Drago, near Plaza de la Constitucíon, Icod de los Vinos 🏛 Inexpensive 🍴 Bars and cafés nearby (€) 🚌 107, 108, 325 ❓ Icod holds a Dragon Tree Festival in Sep

3 El Teide

www.telefericoteide.com

The highest mountain in Spain is an active but sleeping volcano, soaring majestically above the island it helped create.

Before the Spanish conquest, the Guanche people of the Canary Islands revered this conical mountain crested with snow and fire. For a century or so at a stretch the volcano remains dormant. The most recent eruption was a small one in 1898, and some noises have been issuing from it of late. Scientists are monitoring any risk.

Over the millennia, El Teide's eruptions have added more and more land to the island, albeit in the form of a blasted landscape of twisted rock and debris. But it's a scene that thrills visitors, and the region is now protected within the Parque Nacional del Teide (➤ 138–140). Although it's not particularly accessible, and offers nothing but its dignified presence, El Teide is first among the island's musts.

The original volcano was much larger, but the cone was blown to pieces in a massive eruption and its relics surround Pico del Teide – the summit of El Teide – in a ring of lesser volcanic outlets, known as the Caldera de las Cañadas.

Visits are not always possible. The 3,718m (12,199ft) mountain sometimes guards itself amid mist, snow or powerful winds, even when the weather is fine down on the coast, or swelters in temperatures of 40°C (104°F). However, on fine, calm days experienced, properly equipped hikers can make the 3-hour trek (➤ 72–73), easier on the way up than down (beware of altitude sickness).

Most visitors prefer to take the 8-minute *teleférico* (cable car) ride. Beyond the cable car terminal, there's another 163m (535ft) to climb (150 permits only issued daily, passport needed; see below). Take the climb gently, carry water, wear a sunhat and sunglasses, and bring a light sweater to wear at the summit. The view is dramatic and the experience unforgettable.

✚ 16H ✉ Parque Nacional del Teide 🍴 Cable-car station (refreshments) 🚌 348 from Puerto de la Cruz and 342 from Playa de las Américas depart once daily at 9:15, reaching cable car at 11:15. The 348 returns at 4:15, the 342 at 3:40 (times can vary) ✋ Cable car expensive; hiking free ❓ Cable car hotline ☎ 922 010445 ⚠ Doesn't run in high wind. Last descent 5pm ❓ Permits available from National Park office ✉ Calle Emilio Calzadilla 5, near Plaza del Principe, Santa Cruz ⚠ Mon–Fri 9–2 ☎ 922 290129. Check cable car and weather before setting out

4 Garachico

For 200 years, vessels set sail laden with wine and sugar from Garachico, Tenerife's busiest port. Then in one night the harbour was destroyed.

Created as a port in 1496, the original Garachico became a prosperous colonial town and so it remained for two centuries. Today it is partly buried beneath the present town – on 5 May 1706 the Volcan Negro (south of the town) roared into life, pouring lava through Garachico and into its harbour. The islanders laid out new streets on land formed

by the lava. But the harbour was never to recover, and Garachico, with its fine mansions and cobbled streets, became a handsome relic.

Around Glorieta de San Francisco, the main square, is the old Franciscan monastery, **Convento de San Francisco.** Pre-dating the eruption, it now houses the Casa de la Cultura, hosting events and exhibitions (go in just to see the courtyards and interiors), and Museo de las Ciencias Naturales, a modest mix of local flora, fauna and history – don't miss the pictures showing the route of the lava.

Parque Puerta de Tierra, a lush sunken garden alongside Plaza de Juan González de la Torre, was part of the harbour. A huge arch from the port entrance has been re-erected, and a large wine press in the park also pre-dates the eruption.

For a tremendous view, go up to the roof of **Castillo de San Miguel,** the dark 16th-century fortress that stood firm as the lava flowed past. It contains a little museum and craft stall. Steps lead down to the sea, where rocky pools dot the lava.

✚ 3D ᵰ Isla Baja (€€); Casa Ramón (€) 🚌 107 and 363 (Puerto de la Cruz–Buenavista) hourly ❓ Romería de San Roque, Aug (➤ 25); Feria Artesanía (craft fair) monthly, first Sun. Best view of lava flow is from mountain road to Mirador de Garachico
ℹ Calle Estéban de Ponte 5 ☎ 922 133461

Convento de San Francisco
✉ Glorieta de San Francisco 🕐 Mon–Sat 8–7, Sun 8–2
💰 Inexpensive
Castillo de San Miguel
🕐 Daily 10–6 💰 Inexpensive

5 Loro Parque, Puerto de la Cruz

www.loroparque.com

The premier family attraction on Tenerife is a tropical wildlife zoo that mixes conservation, education and fun.

This is one of the original tourist attractions on Tenerife, located in the island's first holiday resort. From simple beginnings in 1972 as a parrot park (which is what Loro Parque means), it is now an award-winning zoological park, an extravaganza of tropical gardens, a dolphinarium and sea-life centre, with related attractions and rides. Covering 12.5ha (31 acres), with over 2,000 palm trees, it keeps a group of male gorillas for breeding, and has a water zone where the ever-popular sea lions and dolphins seem to relish their role as a holiday entertainment. The park's aquarium tunnel, believed to be the longest in the world, is a transparent underwater

walkway 18.5m (61ft) long. As you walk along, sharks slip through the water, just a few centimetres away. There are flamingos, crocodiles, cranes, giant turtles, jaguars, monkeys and a Nocturnal Bat Cave. Another highlight is the icy Planet Penguin. A special effects cinema, Natura Vision, takes you on a trip through other wildlife centres around the world.

Parrots, however, remain an important element of the park. There are over 300 species living here – the world's largest collection. The birds are being studied, and the park is engaged in important breeding and conservation work. While endangered parrot species may be confined, the more common varieties are used in parrot shows several times each day. These feature clever tricks and elaborate entertainments the parrots have learned.

➕ 6C ✉ 1.5km (1 mile) west of Plaza del Charco near Punta Brava ☎ 922 373841 ⏰ Daily 8:30–6:30 (last admission 4pm) 💷 Expensive 🍴 Choice on site, including a pizzeria (€€) and a self-service buffet (€) 🚌 Free shuttle bus from Avenida de Colón (near Ermita San Telmo) and Plaza del Charco every 20 mins

Los Gigantes

These stupendous sheer cliffs are called The Giants, an apt description of a rock face that soars 600m (1,968ft) from blue sea to blue sky.

One of Tenerife's most breathtaking sights, properly known as Acantilados de los Gigantes, is the soaring dark rock face that rises from the Atlantic to mark the abrupt edge of northwestern Tenerife's Teno Massif. Its sheer grandeur attracts almost all visitors to Tenerife and is best seen from the water. Come by road and join a sightseeing boat when you arrive, or take a boat excursion from one of the resorts. Either way, it's not until you see another boat cruising gently at the foot of these cliffs that their true majesty becomes clear.

The cliffs rise from one end of a pleasant bay called La Canalita. At the other end there's a small resort with a quiet, civilized feel and a black sand beach called Playa de los Guios. Slightly remote, it preserves a calm atmosphere now rare on the island and the cliffs and the sea prevent much expansion. South of Los Gigantes, however, the coast has been heavily developed, mostly with apartment blocks. An excellent black sand beach, Playa de la Arena, near Puerto de Santiago creates a focal point.

✚ 13H ✉ 2km (1.2 miles) from Puerto de Santiago
🍴 Bars and restaurants near the marina (€–€€) 🚍 325 (Puerto de la Cruz) or 473 to the south coast resorts
🚢 Excursions from Puerto de Santiago, Playa de las Américas and Los Cristianos ℹ️ Edificio Seguro del Sol Avenida Marítima 36–37, Playa de la Arena ☎ 922 860348

7 Mercado Nuestra Señora de África, Santa Cruz

Tenerife's main produce market, the Market of Our Lady of Africa, is a dazzle of colour and energy, a picture of the island's abundance.

The generosity of the Canaries and their surrounding ocean, and their ready access to all the abundance of the rest of Spain, are daily apparent in the wonderful displays in this lively and atmospheric enclosed market. Flowers fill the eye, alongside colourful heaps of fruit and vegetables, and other stalls laden with fish and meat. You'll find small live animals, a multitude of farm cheeses made of cow's, sheep's or goat's milk (sometimes all three) and honey. Traders sell cheap cassettes and CDs, often of foot-stamping Spanish and Latin American music. Interestingly, all is neat and orderly, with a surprising level of efficiency.

The market is near the heart of the old quarter of Santa Cruz, not far from the lanes of a red-light district, and usually spills out into these surrounding streets, where stalls sell kitchenware, fabrics and household items. The market entrance is a circular arch leading straight to the flower stalls. Beyond lies a veritable bazaar within the central courtyard.

There's officially no market on Sunday, but that's when the big weekly *rastro* sets up outside the market hall, a mixed craft and flea market with an array of stallholders from home and abroad selling plenty of genuine high-quality arts and crafts, but also a hotch-potch of cheap souvenirs, second-rate factory-made 'craft' items, leather goods, assorted cast-offs and second-hand items. For philatelists several stallholders specialize in stamps.

🕀 *Santa Cruz 4e* ✉ Just off Calle de San Sebastián, at the south end of Puente Servador, Santa Cruz ☎ 922 214743 🕐 Mon–Sat 6–3 (Sun *rastro* 10–2) ❓ Watch for pickpockets who prey on tourists

8 Museo de Antropología de Tenerife

A fascinating collection of Canary Islands folk culture, housed in a fine restored country mansion, one of the most beautiful buildings on the island.

The Casa de Carta, a beautiful, low Canarian farmhouse and country mansion, dates back to the end of the 17th century, and is one of Tenerife's prettiest architectural gems. The building is an exquisite arrangement of carved wooden doors, balconies, porticoes and patios. It stands among tropical gardens in the countryside overlooking the village of Valle de Guerra.

For centuries the home of the Carta family of regional administrators, the building now houses

the important Tenerife Anthropology Museum (or MAT). Reconstructed rooms reveal much about rural life in Tenerife, and there are examples of all the island's folk arts and crafts. Inside, 14 exhibition rooms are used to recreate appealing little glimpses of ordinary life in past times. The principal displays are of weaving, needlework and pottery, as well as farm tools, fabrics, clothing, ceramics and furniture.

The most interesting exhibits are of traditional Canarian dress from the 18th century onwards, highlighting the small but important differences of style and colour between one island and the next. Embroidered and patterned festival clothes, wedding clothes and everyday workwear are on show. The weaving and sewing rooms show how these clothes would have been made in the past.

🚩 8B ✉ On road TF-16 between Valle de Guerra and Tacoronte, about 25km (15.5 miles) from Puerto de la Cruz ☎ 922 546300 🕓 Tue–Sun 9–7. Open only during exhibitions which are usually taking place 💷 Moderate (Sun free) 🍴 In and around nearby Tacoronte (€€) 🚌 Call Tacoronte Bus Information ☎ 922 561807

9 Nuestra Señora de la Concepción, La Laguna

When Guanche leaders were 'persuaded' to become Christian and submit to Spanish rule, they were brought to this grandiose church to be baptized.

The island's oldest church, with much outstanding craftsmanship, Our Lady of the Immaculate Conception represents a landmark in Canarian history and has the status of a Spanish national shrine. Its greatest claim to fame is that the big glazed 16th-century baptismal font, brought here from Seville, was used to 'convert' defeated Guanche warriors to Christianity. You'll find it in the *baptisterio* (baptistery) set to one side of the main entrance, with family trees displayed above.

Though much changed since its foundation in 1502, even in those days the church was extraordinarily grand for a far-flung colony, with elaborately carved gilded wooden ceiling panels in Moorish design. Over the centuries, the church benefited from the finest workmanship on the island, its Gothic origins becoming overlaid with Renaissance style and then baroque decoration.

The triple-nave church has probably the grandest and richest interior on Tenerife, and rivals any other building in the Canaries. The gold and silver paint and metalwork are breathtaking, together with rich 17th-century and later retables. Immediately obvious on entering the building, the extravagant woodcarving of the 18th-century pulpit is considered one of the best examples in Spain. The choir stalls, too, are beautifully carved.

The eye-catching seven-storey tower, dating from the 17th century, has a distinctive Moorish look and is the main landmark of this historic town.

✚ 9B ✉ Plaza del la Concepción, La Laguna 🕑 Daily 9–1, 5:30–8 👋 Inexpensive 🍴 *Tapas* bars and restaurants nearby 🚌 101, 102, 103 (Puerto de la Cruz or Santa Cruz–La Laguna) every 30 mins

10 Pirámides de Güímar

www.piramidesdeguimar.net

The discovery and restoration of Tenerife's intriguing pyramids has caused international academic interest, and raised questions about the spread of pyramid culture in ancient times.

High on the edge of the steep east-coast town of Güímar, six of Tenerife's curious little step-pyramids stand within an attractive and informative **Parque Etnográfico** (Ethnographic Park), with a museum and visitor centre, Casa de Chacona.

The Pirámides de Güímar, first excavated by Norwegian archaeologist-explorer Thor Heyerdahl during the 1990s, are broad, flat ceremonial platforms arranged on the tops of stepped stone structures. Very similar to the pyramids of Peru and

Mexico, but on a smaller scale, they also have similarities with the pyramids of Mesopotamia, which pre-date those of Egypt. The Güímar pyramids are aligned with the movement of the sun at the summer and winter solstices.

Ancient Güímar was important to the Guanches, and the chieftain at Güímar had high status – still true when Spanish colonists first settled here. In records of the Spanish conquerors, there is only a brief mention of these structures. The native people were regarded with such contempt that little note was made of their religion and rituals, and they were soon wiped out,

It now seems the Guanches may have been a surviving remnant of the prehistoric pyramid culture that appeared around 4,500 years ago in Egypt and Mesopotamia, and at almost the same time among the Incas of South America. Mummifying the dead was another unusual custom shared by ancient Egypt, the Incas of Peru and the Guanches of Tenerife. Transatlantic sailors to this day pause at the Canaries before the long journey to the Americas, and it seems that voyagers of ages past did the same. Their mysterious pyramids also contribute evidence to a theory that the Guanches were originally Berbers from North Africa.

✚ 8E ✉ 23km (14 miles) south of Santa Cruz; 3km (2 miles) inland from coastal highway; to reach the Ethnographic Park follow signs to 'Pirámides'

Parque Etnográfico

☎ 922 514510 🕓 Daily 9:30–6 💷 Moderate 🍴 Snack bar and souvenir shop on site (€) 🚌 120, 121, 124 – 30 mins direct from Santa Cruz

Best things to do

Top beaches

El Médano
Disregard the nearby sprawl of gleaming apartment buildings and you'll find yourself on one of the best natural beaches in Tenerife, with around 3km (2 miles) of pale sands. The fact that it's in a windy spot on the island's southeastern coast is no disadvantage – it attracts windsurfing devotees from around the world (➤ 157).

Los Cristianos
The original mass-market resort became popular for good reason: Los Cristianos has one of the best beaches on the island, the huge and attractive golden sands of Playa de las Vistas, west of the busy port. The second sandy beach, Playa de los Cristianos, is east of the port. Both are backed by promenades with shops and budget eateries and offer water sports and boat excursions (➤ 154).

Playa de las Américas, Costa Adeje
Focal point of the southern resorts, the main beach area of Playa de las Américas is divided into sections improved with imported sand and protected by breakwaters of dark volcanic boulders. To the south are 'unimproved' beaches of rock and shingle (➤ 155).

Playa del Camisón
This very attractive, soft sandy beach, backed by a tree-lined promenade and grassy verges and with a beach restaurant at one end, lies in front of the Mare Nostrum Resort (➤ 155).

Playa del Duque
A pleasant, gentle, fairly small bay of pale soft sand, with cafés and the Hotel del Duque behind, and close to the upmarket Plaza del Duque area, this is Costa Adeje's smartest beach (➤ 152).

Playa Fañabé
Costa Adeje's main beach is a long sandy stretch with bars, restaurants and shops close by (➤ 152).

Playa Jardín
Puerto de la Cruz doesn't have any good beaches, but this attractively laid-out bay of black sand, west of the town centre, is a popular spot for swimming and sunbathing (➤ 128).

Playa de las Teresitas
Saharan sand was imported to improve this lovely beach just north of Santa Cruz, and an area with palm trees gives it an exotic feel and some much-needed shade. A breakwater makes for sheltered swimming. Weekdays are surprisingly uncrowded (➤ 111).

Places to have lunch

Casa del Vino La Baranda (€€)
Enjoy excellent *tapas* and island wines on the terrace of this delightful 17th-century country house – now a wine museum.
✉ Autopista del Norte, km 21 (El Sauzal) ☎ 922 563886

El Monasterio (€€)
In the hilly countryside behind Puerto de la Cruz, this charming, rustic place is set in a former convent.
✉ La Montañeta, Los Realejos ☎ 922 344311

La Cava (€€)
Unusual in this touristy zone, La Cava gives a chance to enjoy authentic Spanish cooking in a pleasant outdoor atmosphere.
✉ Calle El Cabezo 22, Los Cristianos ☎ 922 790493

La Langostera (€–€€)
A tempting little fish restaurant where you can enjoy the freshest of simple Canarian cuisine.
✉ Paseo Marítimo, Los Abrigos ☎ 922 170302

Las Rocas (€€€)

The beach club of the Hotel Jardín Tropical provides one of the most enjoyable lunchtime experiences on the south coast. The speciality is high-quality seafood.

✉ Calle Gran Bretaña, Costa Adeje ☎ 922 750000

Los Roques (€€)

A relaxed, comfortable and attractive boat-deck-style restaurant by the waterfront of the fishing harbour, this is the place to enjoy good imaginative food.

✉ Calle La Marina 16, Los Abrigos ☎ 922 749401 🕓 Closed Sun and Mon

Los Troncos (€€)

One of the best restaurants in the Tenerife capital, noted for its high standard of traditional Canarian cooking.

✉ Calle General Goded 17, Santa Cruz ☎ 922 284152

Otelo (€)

Beautifully located at the very top of the town, right at the start of the Barranco del Infierno walk, this unpretentious country diner has good food and a wonderful view of sea and hills.

✉ Los Molinos 44, Adeje ☎ 922 780374 🕓 Closed Tue

Parador de la Gomera (€€–€€€)

La Gomera's nicely situated *parador* (1km/0.5 miles from San Sebastián) has a stylish dining room and the best food on the island.

✉ Llano de la Horca, San Sebastián, La Gomera ☎ 922 871100

Parador de las Cañadas del Teide (€€)

The *parador* restaurant is unpretentious, offers good food and is the nearest to El Teide and the major volcanic sites.

✉ Parque Nacional del Teide ☎ 922 374841

Best gardens

Hijuela del Botánico
Although quite small, the garden is a cool oasis of tropical plants, its paths shaded by tall trees and with benches for enjoying it.

✉ Calle Tomás Pérez, La Orotava ☎ 922 330050 🕐 Daily 9–2
✋ Free 🚌 101, 107, 108, 345, 348

Jardín Acuático Risco Bello
Layers of greenery and water cascade from terrace to terrace of pools surrounded by flowers, fruit trees, aquatic plants and flowers, all artistically arranged against the near-vertical slope overlooking Puerto de la Cruz (➤ 124).

Jardín Botánico
Originally built to acclimatize exotic plants and trees brought from tropical climes, this cool, shady respite from the beaches and bustle of Puerto de la Cruz has become a favourite for gardeners and non-gardeners alike (➤ 124–125).

Jardines Marquesado de La Quinta Roja
Well-kept 19th-century gardens cascade colourfully through ravines and onto terraces, into the centre of La Orotava.

✉ Calle San Agustin 🕐 May–Oct 8–10, Nov–Apr 8–9
✋ Moderate 🍽 In the plaza below (€–€€€) 🚌 101, 107, 108, 345, 347, 348

Jardín de Orquideas Sitio Litre
Tenerife's oldest garden has been lovingly cared for by British owners for more than 225 years, and displays a stunning collection of orchids.

✉ Camino del Robado, Puerto de la Cruz ☎ 922 382417
🕐 Daily 9:30–2:30 ✋ Moderate 🍽 Café Orquidea (€)

Jardín Taoro

Adjacent to Jardin Acuático Risco Bello, these steeply terraced gardens in the grounds of the former Hotel Taoro have a waterfall, pools and a bridge. Above is Taoro Park, a large green expanse high above the city.

✉ Carretera Taoro, Puerto de la Cruz ⏱ Daylight hours
✋ Free 🍴 Restaurant-café in gardens (€€)

Mirador de la Garoñona

Showy, colourful flowers and luxuriant trees crown a soaring cliff above the sea, framing coastal views.

✉ Rondo El Sauzelito, El Sauzal ⏱ Thu–Mon 11–10, closed Tue–Wed ✋ Free 🍴 Café Capriccio in gardens (€) 🚌 101

Parque Garciá Sanabria

The broad promenades of this spacious park are lined with flowers; its lawns are decorated by fountains, pools and modern sculpture.

✉ Calle Méndez Nuñez, Santa Cruz ⏱ Daily ✋ Free
🍴 Café (€)

Best festivals

Asunción and Nuestra Señora de la Candelaria
This is an important pilgrimage festival, which involves the whole of Tenerife on 15 August, but has particular meaning in Candelaria.

Candelaria (Candlemas)
This is a big festival and pilgrimage, which takes place on 2 February in certain towns and villages, especially Candelaria.

Carnaval
February is Carnival Month, and the high point of the year for most Tenerife residents is the wild, colourful and sometimes frenzied week-long carnival. It's the second biggest carnival in the world after Rio and draws immense crowds from all Spanish-speaking countries. The climax is Shrove Tuesday, when huge processions

and parades, with participants dressed in fantastic costumes that
have often taken the whole year to prepare, take over the capital
city and to a lesser extent Tenerife's other big towns. The carnival
event in Los Cristianos marks the end of Carnival Month.

Corpus Christi
In late May or early June there are eight days of huge celebrations
throughout the island, especially at La Orotava, La Laguna and
Vilaflor, during which the streets are decorated with sand-and-
flower designs.

Día de las Islas Canarias
Canary Islands Day is celebrated throughout the archipelago on
30 May (▶ 25).

Fiestas del Gran Poder
Puerto de la Cruz comes alive on 15 July, with processions,
parades, fireworks and other celebrations.

Music Festival of the Canary Islands
This January event is a highlight of the Tenerife year, and also
stands out in the list of European festivals. It features world-class
orchestras and solo performers of classical music.

New Year's Eve
At the strike of midnight on New Year's Eve, Tenerife locals have
their own tradition, which is fun to share. At every chime of the
clock you should eat a grape and spit the seeds out. If you can do
that without difficulty, you should also take a sip of *cava* at every
one of the 12 chimes.

Semana Santa (Holy Week)
The celebration of Easter is taken very seriously here, with big,
usually sober, events throughout the island.

Top activities

DIVING

Scuba and offshore diving is popular all around the islands. Several centres offer a good standard and are staffed by qualified instructors. Diving courses should meet PADI standards and you should also check your insurance cover.

GO-KARTING
Karting Club Tenerife

This club has three circuits – one ranked among the best kart circuits in Europe. Several different types of kart are available, including some suitable for children, and there's a viewing terrace and other amusements on site.

✉ Carretera de Cho, at km 66, off the southern Autopista at Guaza

☎ 922 730703

GOLF

Tenerife has some glorious golf courses with stunning scenery, some challenging holes and the luxury of predictably good weather. Top international tournaments have taken place at Golf del Sur, in the south, and nearby Golf Club Las Americas, proud of its environmental awareness, is also recommended. Golf Adeje, also in the south, has an 18-hole and a 9-hole course.

JEEP SAFARIS

To really appreciate the rugged, volcanic landscape of Tenerife without a difficult hike, you can bounce around Mount Teide and other areas in a six-seat, open-top jeep.

SPA

After taking part in any of the energetic pursuits listed above, what could be nicer than a visit to the upmarket Aqua Club Termal in Costa Adeje (Calle Galicia, Torviscas Alto, Adeje, tel: 922 716555), which offers a number of spa and fitness facilities, including a sauna, Turkish bath, a sea-water pool and a huge swimming pool.

SURFING AND WINDSURFING

Near-constant trade winds and warm unpolluted waters ensure ideal conditions for windsurfing and surfing around the island's south coast. One of the best locations is El Médano beach (➤ 58 and 157), close to Reina Sofía Airport, which has hosted world windsurfing championships. Waters on the north coast are often too rough for safe surfing.

WALKING

Graded footpaths marked and maintained by ICONA, the Spanish conservation agency, criss-cross the island. The agency issues a number of maps (available in tourist offices and park visitor centres on the island) showing marked walks. These include a pocket-size pack of 22 different footpath maps, with descriptions in English and some history about each area and the landmarks, flora and fauna. Discovery Walking Guides and Sunflower Guides (available in the UK) are useful additions, aimed at the walker.

Places to shop

African traders
Colourfully dressed West Africans, often Senegalese, hawking on the beaches, in the streets and selling in the markets and fairs of Tenerife add an exotic note. They usually sell very similar goods: leatherwork, carved toys, African drums, beads and, at higher prices, often illegally exported tribal artefacts, including ceremonial masks. Do not buy ivory – it's illegal throughout the EU.

Arguayo
This village is noted for its pottery, which is crafted into rugged pieces without using a potter's wheel. The Centro Alfarero is the place to buy the finished pots.

Casa de los Balcones
Located in the hilltown of La Orotava, this is one of the best-known outlets for the embroidery, lace, pottery and other crafts of the Canary Islands (▶ 36–37 and 148).

Casa del Vino la Baranda
This lovely old farmhouse near El Sauzal offers wine tastings, an interesting film about wine production in Tenerife and, of course, the opportunity to buy (▶ 104) .

Centro de Artesania el Limonero
This is a gourmet delight in Puerto de la Cruz, offering a tempting array of artisan cheeses and wine for sale.

Craft fairs
During the summer *ferias de artesania* are held in many towns, bringing together the island's artisans and artists to showcase their talents.

Mercado Nuestra Señora de Africa
Around 300 stalls at this daily market in Santa Cruz entice

shoppers with their appetizing aromas and range of foodstuffs, including live rabbits and chickens (➤ 48–49).

Parque Nacional de Garajonay, La Gomera
The visitor centre is a terrific place for quality souvenirs. It's an outlet for a variety of island crafts, including banana-leaf baskets, wood carvings and musical instruments (➤ 176–177 and 186).

Pasteleria El Aderno
Don't bother even trying to resist the award-winning island specialities for sale at this wonderful cake shop in Buenavista del Norte.

Rastro
A good way to get to know a place is by seeing what they get rid of. With this in mind, visit the *Rastro* (flea market) at Nuestra Señora de Africa market (➤ 48–49) in Santa Cruz, a lively weekly event on the city streets featuring housewares, clothing and heaps of unnecessary items to arouse your curiosity.

Los Telares
This craft workshop in Hermigua, La Gomera, offers a good range of woven goods, including some lovely handmade rugs (➤ 175).

Places to take the children

Aqualand (Aguapark Octopus)
This water park at Costa Adeje offers slides, pools, dolphin shows and water features (➤ 152).

Camel Park
One of the principal activities at this farm, where camels are bred, is a mini-excursion by camel.
✉ Exit 27 of Autopista del Sur ☎ 922 732422 🕐 Daily 10–5 🚌 Free shuttle bus from Los Cristianos and Playa de las Américas

The Camello Center
There's more fun on camel-back here, with camel rides and donkey safaris followed by tea in an Arab tent.
✉ El Tanque (east of Garachico) ☎ 922 136399 🕐 Daily 10–6

Loro Parque
A tropical wonderland of animals and birds, including parrots, gorillas, tigers, monkeys, penguins, flamingos and performing dolphins (➤ 44–45).

Oasis del Valle
Canarian flora and fauna and other friendly creatures in lush subtropical gardens in the Orotava Valley
✉ El Ramal 35, La Orotava (Exit 33 from Autopista del Norte) ☎ 922 333509 🕐 Daily 10–5 🚌 Free bus from Playa de Martiánez (near Lago), Puerto de la Cruz

Parque Las Aguilas – Jungle Park
You can see condors and crocodiles, tigers, eagles and penguins in this dramatic tropical park. There are five animal display areas, and feeding times are particularly

worth seeing. Also on the site
are dodgem boats and other
amusements (➤ 154).

Parques Exóticos
This cactus and animal park also
has a reptilarium (➤ 160–161).

Pueblo Chico
Models of Canarian landscapes
and buildings are carefully
reproduced to a scale of 1:25 in
this large open-air attraction in
the hills behind Puerto de la Cruz.
🖂 Valle de la Orotava ☎ 922 334060

Tenerife Zoo
Children love the apes and the
other primates here, as well
as the lions, crocodiles and
many other creatures.
🖂 Llano Azul, Arona (Exit 26 of
Autopista del Sur) ☎ 922 751753
🕓 Daily 9:30–6 🚌 Free shuttle bus
from southern resorts

Whale- and dolphin-watching
These are popular activities on
Tenerife, and there are about
20 different species of sea
mammals living in island waters.
Glass-bottomed boats offer a
chance to spot other marine
life too.

up El Teide

The ascent of El Teide is the most exhilarating walk on Tenerife – though it's only suitable for fit, experienced hikers. Take plenty of water and warm clothes, and start as early as possible, checking the weather forecast and that the cable car is running for the return journey (➤ 40–41).

Start from the main road TF-21 at the start of the track to Montaña Blanca.

At first the track passes through a desolate volcanic terrain of sharp, gritty stones. After an hour or an hour and a half, you reach the old Montaña Blanca car park.

Follow the sign indicating the Refugio de Altavista, which starts you on a steeper climb on a sandy track. Climb for about 2 hours along this path to reach the refugio, or mountain refuge – which may or may not be open (usually open daily 5pm to 10am). Continue on the path, the edge of which is clearly marked.

Some 3 hours later, the path becomes stonier, but more level. Eventually you reach the path that leads from the top cable-car station to the summit. To complete the ascent you need a permit (➤ 41).

In a wild landscape of multicoloured volcanic rock and scree, the path becomes a steep scramble.

You'll pass sulphurous steam holes emitting heat and vapour from the ground. The views are phenomenal. The summit is marked by a crucifix, where sometimes elderly local women come to say a prayer, seemingly climbing here with ease.

Return to the cable-car station and take the car down to the road.

Distance 8km (5 miles)
Time 6–7 hours
Start point ✚ 16H. From TF-21 Montaña Blanca bus stop
End point ✚ 16H. Top cable-car station (La Rambleta), or the summit
Lunch Take a picnic – no food or water en route. There is a bar at La Rambleta (€)

Best churches

Basilica de Nuestra Señora de la Candelaria, Candelaria
Dedicated to the patron saint of the Canary Islands, and containing
a fine statue of the Virgin, this huge modern church overlooking
the sea is surrounded by legends and mythology (➤ 102–104).

Iglesia de Nuestra Señora de la Concepción, Santa Cruz
A prominent city landmark, this church (➤ 86–87) was extensively
restored in the late 20th century. It has many historic associations,
and is fronted by an attractive plaza.

**Iglesia de Nuestra Señora de la Peña de Francia,
Puerto de la Cruz**
This dignified building is the principal church in Puerto de la Cruz
and dates back to the 1680s (➤ 123). It has some fine statuary, an
ornate altarpiece and a 19th-century organ from London.

Iglesia de San Francisco, Santa Cruz
This is a place of contrasts, with a charmingly simple structure but
a plethora of elaborate decoration inside. It was built in 1680 as
part of a Roman Catholic monastery (➤ 87).

Iglesia de San Pedro, Vilaflor
This imposing 17th-century church is dedicated to the town's most
famous son, Brother Peter, who later founded the Order of
Bethlehem in Guatemala.

Iglesia de la Virgen de la Asunción, San Sebastian, La Gomera
The main attraction of this church is a mural that shows a battle
with, and defeat of, British pirates in 1743.

Nuestra Señora de la Concepción, La Laguna
A grandiose church, the oldest (1502) on the island. Inside and
out it is a glorious testament to the outstanding talents of island
craftsmen (➤ 52–53).

Best buys

Embroidery, lace and threadwork
The Canaries are known for exquisite embroidery *(bordados)* and fine threadwork *(calados)*, created by patient and skilful local women – beware of street sellers and market traders offering inferior, low-priced, imported factory-made work, claiming that it is local craftwork. Vilaflor is known for handmade lace.

Food and drink
Super-sweet *cobana* (banana liqueur) in banana-shaped bottles makes a novel souvenir, or you could take home a bottle of *mojo* sauce. There are also prettily packaged sweets and biscuits, honey or the *miel de palma* (palm syrup) produced on La Gomera.

Leatherwork
The whole of Spain is famous for its leatherwork, and there's no shortage of quality items in Tenerife shops.

Music
You'll find recorded Canarian folk music at some markets and craft centres, or you can buy a traditional musical instrument – the stringed *timple*, perhaps, or castanets.

Pottery
Canarian potters traditionally didn't use a wheel, and highly skilled local potters still produce distinctive household objects and decorative items. Look in the craft shops for *gánigos* – household pots – and jewellery decorated with Guanche symbols.

Unusual souvenirs
Among more unusual purchases are items made from palm leaves, or banana-leaf baskets. Dragon trees are available in souvenir shops, but are only suitable for a frost-free environment. A better choice (but not for US or Canadian visitors) would be the 'bird of paradise' flowers that come packaged for freight.

Wickerwork
Local handmade basketwork is distinctive and pretty, and makes a good choice for souvenirs. Skilled basket-weavers can be seen working in the many craft fairs.

Woodcrafts
Native wood is fashioned into bowls, dishes and spoons, or there are items made by Tenerife craftspeople from imported olive wood.

Duty-free goods
The Canary Islands are a duty-free area, so perfumes, cameras, binoculars, CD players and electronic goods can be bought at lower prices than at home (though there's a 5 per cent local IGIC tax). In major towns and resorts Asian-run 'bazaars' are the usual outlet and marked prices may be open to a bit of haggling.

Boat trips

Game fishing
Anglers will enjoy the big-game fishing trips, in the hope of hauling in a shark, tuna or swordfish.

Glass-bottomed boats
These offer an excellent way to enjoy the Canarian marine life for those who can't or don't want to scuba dive.

La Gomera
The boat trip to La Gomera is by far the best of many available on Tenerife. It's a full day, with the option of a coach tour of La Gomera or renting a car to explore independently.

Nashira Uno
Excursions from the yacht harbour in Los Gigantes cruise up to the massive cliff of Los Gigantes for a better view than you can get from the land. Trips often include whale-watching.

Nostramo

A beautiful Spanish schooner built in 1918 takes you out to see dolphins and whales, with an unforgettable lunch stop below Los Gigantes and a pause in Masca Bay for a swim.

✉ Playa San Juan, Playa de las Américas ☎ 922 750085 (Playa de las Américas); 922 385116 (Puerto de la Cruz) 🕐 Departs daily 10am

Los Órganos

From La Gomera you can take a boat trip to see Los Órganos, a series of slender, hexagonal basalt columns that rise 80m (262ft) off the north coast. They can only be seen from the sea.

Pirate cruises

What better reason for a cruise than simply having fun. These cruises usually include a barbecue on a quiet beach and a swim.

Lady Shelley

This glass-bottomed catamaran excursion from Los Cristianos to Masca (5 hours) or La Caleta (3 hours) is a simple fun outing with swimming, sunbathing, music and a leisurely lunch on board. You usually see some whales and dolphins too.

✉ Pirámide de Arona ☎ 922 757549; www.ladyshelley.com

Tropical Delfin and *Royal Delfin*

These modern excursion boats have underwater windows so that passengers can view the sea life.

✉ South Pier, Puerto Colón, Playa de las Américas ☎ 900 700709 🕐 Daily trips 10:30, 1:30

Whale-watching

The waters around the island are home to about 200 pilot whales, often best seen between Los Cristianos and Los Gigantes, and you often see dolphins, too. Make sure you only go with a properly licensed company that will observe the regulations.

Places to be entertained

Auditorio de Tenerife

Santiago Calatrava's astounding, somewhat surreal concert hall soars over the shoreline of Santa Cruz, providing a world-class venue for classical music and dance (➤ 116–117).

✉ Avenida Constitución 1, Santa Cruz de Tenerife ☎ 922 568600; www.auditoriodetenerife.com

Barbacoa Tacoronte

If you miss Tenerife's famous carnival, try to catch this folklore show, which is based on the event, with colourful costumes and a barbecue-style dinner.

✉ Calle Las Tocas 99, Tacoronte ☎ 922 382910

Casino Taoro

In a lofty parkland setting at the back of town, this is an elegant building where you can enjoy cocktails, fine dining and, of course, playing the tables. You will need to dress smartly and bring your passport (➤ 149).

✉ Parque Taoro 22, Puerto de la Cruz ☎ 922 380550 🕐 8pm–4am

Castillo San Miguel

If you enjoy medieval banquets, sample the Canarian version here, dining to the accompaniment of jousting tournaments, singing, dancing and music. The castillo is also the setting for many other fun entertainments. It's located in the hills east of Los Cristianos and above the Costa del Silencio area (➤ 172).

✉ San Miguel Aldea Blanca (exit 24 from Autopista del Sur) ☎ 922 700276

Pirámide de Arona

This lavish venue is part of the Mare Nostrum Resort. It contains an excellent restaurant where several times a week opera singers stroll among the diners; beneath it, one of the largest and best theatres on the island stages a top-quality musical every evening.

✉ Playa de las Américas ☎ 922 757549

Sala Alhambra

Highly trained Andalucian horses perform an intricate 'ballet' to music. This form of dressage is a specialty of these horses and riders, many of whom are trained at the Royal Andalucian School of Equestrian Art in Jerez de la Frontera. Shows take place at an authentic Canarian farmhouse; some include typical meals.

✉ Camino del Coche, Esquilon Bajo, Puerta de la Cruz ☎ 922 385390
🚌 345, 347, 348 ✋ Expensive

Teatro Guimerá

The plays (in Spanish) might only appeal to those with a very good grasp of the language, but you can also see opera, ballet and classical concerts here (➤ 117).

✉ Plaza Isla de la Madera ☎ 922 364603; 922 606923

Tenerife Palace

International performers play this cabaret spot and you can enjoy dinner while you see a glitzy show (➤ 150).

✉ Camino del Coche, Puerto de la Cruz ☎ 922 382960

Exploring

Tenerife is a year-round holiday playground, with 4 million visitors annually, but it is also an island with a fascinating history and a rich cultural life. It has a landscape that's well worth exploring, from lush banana farms to dense forests to the moonscape of its volcanic heart. Modern tourist resorts have brought greenery, enterprise and life to the arid south, with their hotel and apartment blocks and fine beaches of imported sand. Tourism may have negative aspects, but it has brought prosperity, and occupies land that was once barren and unproductive.

Tenerife has some fine architecture, from splendid old churches to the stunning modern Auditorio; it has excellent museums, superb craftwork, tasty cuisine and local wines. This is a place that deserves some careful planning and selective exploration to uncover hidden secrets that many tourists will never find.

The North

The real life of Tenerife is all in the north. Here the whole history of Tenerife can be told, for the Guanches mainly occupied the northern half, and the Spanish too settled and cultivated this area. Until package holidays took off in the 1960s, even holidaymakers rarely ventured south of Puerto de la Cruz, except for the essential excursion to the summit of El Teide. As a result, almost all of the island's art, culture, its Spanish colonial legacy, and its best sightseeing, are in the north.

Santa Cruz de Tenerife

The climate is responsible for this: the north and northwest, facing the trade winds, catch all of Tenerife's gentle rain. Parts of this fertile half of the island are exotically verdant, with tropical flowers and greenery. That's what attracted the first aristocratic tourists, who adored the permanent springtime, rich crops and lush garden landscape of northern Tenerife.

SANTA CRUZ DE TENERIFE

Santa Cruz, the island's capital, still has the authentic feel and look of colonial Spain. It's not a holiday resort, but a vibrant Latin city where many Tinerfeños live and work. The name means Holy Cross of Tenerife, and comes from the crucifix planted boldly at this spot by the ruthless Spanish conqueror Alonso Fernández de Lugo, when he strode ashore in 1493 with 1,000 men to take possession of the Guanches' island home.

During the five centuries since the conquest, Santa Cruz has remained the focal point of Tenerife's culture and history. While the gaudy, multicultural Tenerife of modern tourism stays way down south, the resolutely Spanish capital has remained almost unaffected by the millions of package-holiday visitors.

Only tourists determined to know and understand the island, and looking for something more than a suntan, choose to stay here. It's also due to the diverse economy of the capital, with its oil processing, waterfront industry and deep-water harbour. Now though, Santa Cruz has polished up some of its treasures and even provides a jaunty little 'train' to take people on a tour of the sights. At the same time, holidaymakers have realized there's more to Tenerife than *bierkellers* and beaches, and that some of the best sightseeing is in and around Santa Cruz. The waterfront area and nearby streets are the city's focal point for locals and visitors alike.

➕ 10C 🛈 Palacio Insular (ground floor), Plaza de España ☎ 922 239592
🕐 Mon–Fri 8–6, Sat 9–1

Iglesia de Nuestra Señora de la Concepción

One of the city's most important landmarks, the Church of Our Lady of the Conception is also one of its most significant historical monuments. Its attractive square tower rises from a plaza enclosed by whitewashed 19th-century buildings (including the handsome exterior of the tobacco works, Tinerfeña Fabrica de Tabacos). Begun in 1502, and much changed in the 17th and 18th

centuries, the church was extensively restored during the 1990s. The cross which de Lugo first placed on Tenerife soil has been kept here, as has the British flag captured from one of Nelson's ships during his 1797 raid. An additional feature of this fine church is the tomb of Nelson's opponent, General Gutierrez, defender of Santa Cruz.

✠ *Santa Cruz 5e* 🖂 Plaza de la Iglesia 🕐 Daily 9–1, 5:30–8 ✋ Free 🍴 Nearby in Plaza de la Candelaria (€€)

Iglesia de San Francisco

The delightful Church of St Francis combines simplicity with elaborate, abundant decoration. Most striking are the wooden ceiling, a painted arch, a fine organ and two baroque *retablos* (altarpieces) dating from the 17th and 18th centuries. To the right of the high altar is a separate chapel with a Moorish-style ceiling. The church, built in 1680, was originally part of the Franciscan monastery of San Pedro de Alcántara, said to have been founded by Irish refugees fleeing from Elizabeth I's anti-Catholic tyranny. The monastery no longer exists, but the buildings now house the Municipal Fine Arts Museum (► 89); the square in which it stands was once the friary garden.

✠ *Santa Cruz 5c* 🖂 Calle Villalba Hervás 🕐 Mon–Fri 9–1, 5:30–8 ✋ Free 🍴 Café del Príncipe (► 114–115)

Mercado Nuestra Señora de África

Best places to see, ➤ 48–49.

Museo Militar Regional de Canarias

Todo por la Patria – All for the Fatherland – is the inscription above the gateway into this collection of important relics from the military past of the Canary Islands. Housed in part of the semicircular 19th-century barracks, Cuartel de Almeida, the Canaries Regional Military Museum is proud and patriotic in tone. The oldest exhibits are the weapons used by the Guanches against the Spanish.

Among various later insignia and memorabilia, a highlight of the collection is El Tigre, the cannon used to defend Santa Cruz against Nelson's 1797 attack and believed to be responsible for the loss of his right arm. Flags taken from one of Nelson's defeated ships, HMS *Emerald*, are also displayed. Even more compelling is the small section devoted to General Francisco Franco, dictator of Spain from 1936 to 1975. You can see his desk, plans and a photograph of him with supporters pledging allegiance at Las Raíces, near La Esperanza. A map shows the route of the plane *Dragon Rapide*, which flew from Croydon in southern England to Tenerife, picked up the future dictator and took him to Morocco, from where he launched his coup.

✚ *Santa Cruz 6a* ✉ Calle San Isidro 2 ☎ 922 843500 ⏰ Tue–Sun 10–2
✋ Free ❓ Remember to take your passport to the Muséo Militar – you probably won't be admitted without it

Museo Municipal de Bellas Artes

Tenerife's excellent Municipal Fine Arts Museum was opened in 1900. Together with the city library, it is housed in the pleasant setting of a former Franciscan monastery. The 10 busts lined up outside are of Tenerife artists, musicians, writers and thinkers. Inside, the collection on two storeys includes the work of Canarian artists, several of historical interest, and more distinguished European works mainly covering the 17th to 19th centuries. Most interesting are the frequent temporary exhibitions of works loaned by Spain's leading museums of art.

 *Santa Cruz 5c* ✉ Calle José Murphy 12, Plaza del Príncipe ☎ 922 244358 🕐 Tue–Fri 10–8, Sat–Sun 10–3 ✋ Free 🍴 Café del Príncipe (➤ 114–115)

Museo de la Naturaleza y El Hombre

This worthy museum, situated in a most attractive former hospital with a galleried courtyard, deals seriously but accessibly with the archaeology, anthropology and ethnography of the Canary Islands, as well as the natural history. The establishment is essentially two museums in one – Nature and Man being dealt with separately – and is split in half, naturally following the plan of the building. Archaeology and the history of the Canaries lie on the left of the entrance and the fauna and flora of the islands on the right. Ten distinct sections tackle these different aspects of the Canary Islands with displays as varied as African and pre-Columbian art, aboriginal therapy, the Canaries during the Spanish Conquest and the Canary Islands today.

The main emphasis is placed on the islands' pre-Hispanic history and culture. Much of the evidence of Guanche culture relates to burial, and the museum displays fascinating material from Guanche tombs and burial sites. Some dramatic exhibits include Guanche preserved bodies in a display on mummification, as well as skeletons and hundreds of skulls, some of them trepanned (with drilled holes). Interesting too, though less dramatic, are the displays of Guanche household items, pottery, tools and body decorations, as well as indigenous Canarian plant and animal life.

➕ *Santa Cruz 5e* ✉ Calle Fuente Morales ☎ 922 209320 🕐 Tue–Sun 9–7
🖐 Moderate (Sun free) 🍴 Nearby in Plaza de la Candelaria

Parque Marítimo César Manrique

When the Cabildo (Island Council) wanted to do something with the unsightly disused industrial dockyards near the old Castillo de San Juan, they commissioned the brilliant Canarian artist and designer César Manrique to work on the project. His brief was very limited, but even so Manrique managed to redesign the docklands site into an attractive leisure complex linking the sea with the Castillo.

The Castillo dates back to 1641, and was part of the town's defences (the Castillo San Cristóbal was located where the Plaza de España lies now). It was once a marketplace for African slaves.

Today the Parque Marítimo is a pleasant lido, with palms and sunbathing terraces situated around a beautiful seawater pool (similar to the Lago Martiánez César Manrique created for Puerto de la Cruz, ➤ 126).

To the east of the fort lies the town's striking Auditorio. Designed like a sea shell by Santiago Calatrava, it is Santa Cruz's main concert hall (➤ 116–117). Southwards stretches a huge palm park (Palmetum), still being planted, while across the busy coastal highway is a large, eye-catching exhibition space for trade fairs and conferences.

✚ *Santa Cruz 5f (off map)*/10C ✉ Avenida de la Constitución ☎ 922 203244 ◷ Daily 10–6 ✋ Moderate 🍴 Choice on site (€–€€€) 🚌 909 and others along Avenida de la Constitución

Parque Municipal García Sanabria

This delightful 6ha (15-acre) park full of shrubs, trees, exotic flowers, fountains and tranquil corners is the largest – and probably the most beautiful – urban park in the Canaries. Popular with locals, it was laid out in the 1920s and is named after the mayor of that time. He is honoured by a large monument in the centre of the park.

The somewhat incongruous pieces of modern sculpture are the product of an international street sculpture competition held in 1973. There is also a zoo, a play area and an intriguing floral clock. Take a break on the tiled benches, stroll the gravel pathways or get a snack at one of the little kiosks.

✚ *Santa Cruz 4b* ✉ Off Rambla del General Franco 👤 Free 🍴 Snacks available at park kiosks (€) 🚌 Town buses along Rambla del General Franco

Plaza de España

A large square near the waterfront, this spacious plaza is the heart of the city. The whole square was formerly the site of the principal Santa Cruz fortification, Castillo San Cristóbal, demolished in 1929. Here now stands the grimly imposing Franco-era Palacio Insular, seat of the Cabildo or Island Council, built in the then popular Rationalist style. The huge central Monumento de los Caidos, Monument to the Fallen, honours local people who fell in war, including the Spanish Civil War – Franco's manifesto was broadcast from here. The monument is flanked by statues of two *menceys* (Guanche chieftains).

✚ *Santa Cruz 6d* ✉ Off Avenida de José Antonio Primo de Rivera
🍴 Bars and cafés nearby (€–€€)

Plaza de la Candelaria

This pleasant traffic-free square has good bars and shops, including an *artesanía* (craft shop). Centuries ago, it was the entrance to the vanished Castillo San Cristóbal, once one of the two main defences of the town (the other was Castillo San Juan), and here the island's troops would parade and be inspected. The centrepiece of the plaza is the appealing baroque statue of Our

Lady of Candelaria, holding the infant Jesus and a tall candle. Formerly known as Plaza del Castillo, the square acquired its new name along with the statue.

At No 9, the Banco Español de Credito occupies the old Palacio de Carta: behind a rather dull facade this is a fine 18th-century mansion with carved wooden balconies and an elegant patio, immaculately restored by the bank. Originally built as the family home of Captain Matías Carta, it is now one of the best examples of traditional Canarian domestic architecture. Open during bank hours, it deserves a look inside – perhaps when you need to change money.

✚ *Santa Cruz 6d* ✉ West of Plaza de España
🍴 Bars and cafés in the square (€–€€)

a walk around Santa Cruz

Start in the waterfront Plaza de España (➤ 92–93), dominated by its Civil War memorial and the massive Palacio Insular, housing the tourist office and Tenerife's council (Cabildo).

Walk into the adjoining square, Plaza de la Candelaria.

This agreeable pedestrianized square (➤ 93) has good bars, craft shops and sights, including the Banco Español de Credito in the charming 18th-century Palacio de Carta.

At the end of the square, continue on Calle del Castillo.

This is the main shopping street of Santa Cruz, a lively, colourful avenue of little shops with gaudy signs, 'bazaars' and mingled crowds of tourists and locals.

Continue to Plaza de Weyler.

There's an Italian white marble fountain at the centre of this popular square. To one side stands the Capitanía General, where Franco lived while he was based here.

At the northern tip of the square, turn along Calle Méndez Núñez.

This less interesting street soon leads to the Parque Municipal García Sanabria (➤ 92), an enjoyable green space away from street noise where you can relax on the tiled benches.

Take Calle del Pilar, opposite the park's south side. Follow this street to Plaza del Príncipe.

In the square, once the garden of a monastery, laurel trees shade a bandstand. To one side the Museo Municipal de Bellas Artes (➤ 89) occupies the former monastery, alongside the Iglesia de San Francisco (➤ 87).

Calle de Béthencourt leads the short distance back to Plaza de España.

Distance 3km (2 miles)
Time 1 hour walking, plus 2 hours sightseeing
Start/end point Plaza de España ✚ *Santa Cruz 6d*
Lunch Café del Príncipe (➤ 114–115)

LA LAGUNA

Outwardly unappealing, the island's second city is a big, sprawling settlement that is rapidly spreading towards Santa Cruz, which is only 8km (5 miles) away. In common with the capital, La Laguna also has a life and an economy that does not depend upon tourism. A large number of islanders work in the city, and there's also a thriving university, which gives the town a lively, youthful Spanish energy.

La Laguna dates back to 1496, when *conquistador* Alonso Fernández de Lugo set it up as the island's capital, which it remained until 1723. The name means The Lagoon, but there is no lagoon here now (the town is properly known as San Cristóbal de la Laguna). The secret of the town is its exquisite historic quarter, where many fine 16th- and 17th-century Renaissance mansions survive.

It is rewarding to take a leisurely walk around the old quarter. To see most of the sights, stroll along Calle Obispo Rey Redondo from Plaza del Adelantado to Iglesia de Nuestra Señora de la Concepción (➤ 52–53), and back along parallel Calle San Agustín.
🚩 9B

Ayuntamiento (Town Hall)

At the start of Calle Obispo Rey Redondo, La Laguna's town hall or *ayuntamiento* is a charming building in Tenerife style. Originally constructed in the 16th century, it was rebuilt in 1822 with fine wooden panelling and a Moorish-style window. Inside, murals illustrate key events from the island's past, and the flag that Alonso Fernández de Lugo placed on Tenerife soil has been displayed here. Next door, Casa de los Capitánes Generales (House of the Captain Generals), built in 1624, was once the impressive residence of the island's military commanders. Now it is used as an exhibition space.

✉ Calle Obispo Rey Redondo 🍴 In Plaza del Adelantado (€)
ℹ Plaza del Adelantado ☎ 922 631194

Calle San Agustín

In this delightful old-fashioned street look for the Instituto de Canarias Cabrera Pinto (Institute of Canarian Studies), noted for its exquisite traditional patio and handsome bell tower. The fine 17th-century facade next door, of the San Agustín monastery, is an empty shell – the building was destroyed by fire in 1963.

🖂 Calle San Agustín 🍴 In Plaza del Adelantado (€)

Catedral

The town's large cathedral is older than it appears. Founded in 1515, it was subsequently enlarged and a neoclassical facade was added in 1813. This last feature survives but the remainder was radically rebuilt during the early 20th century. Nevertheless, the dim interior contains a gilded baroque retable, while set back from the high altar is the modest tomb of the island's conqueror and the town's founder, Alonso Fernández de Lugo, buried here in 1525.

🖂 Plaza de la Catedral 🕐 Mon–Sat 8–1, 5–7:30. Sun open for Mass only
👆 Free

Iglesia Convento Santa Catalina

The latticework gallery of the Santa Catalina Convent Church,
beside the town hall, is one of several attractive architectural
features. Inside, the former convent church has a silver-covered
altar and baroque *retablos*. Notice the little revolving hatch near the
side entrance in Calle Dean Palahi, used by mothers who once
wished to abandon their newborn girl babies by 'donating' them
anonymously to the convent, to be brought up as nuns.

✉ Plaza del Adelantado 🕐 Mon–Sat 7–11:45, Sun 6:30–8 💷 Free
🍴 In Plaza del Adelantado (€)

Iglesia de Nuestra Señora de la Concepción

Best places to see, ➤ 52–53.

Museo de la Ciencia y el Cosmos

The fascinating and entertaining Museum of Science and the
Cosmos sets out to show the connection between man and the
earth, and between the earth and the rest of the universe. With a

variety of hands-on exhibits
and displays, visitors learn
about galaxies, our solar
system and the human body,
complete with such diversions
as listening to the sound of a
baby in the womb, taking a lie-
detector test and watching a
skeleton ride a bicycle.

✉ Calle Via Láctea, off the La
Cuesta road, near the university
☎ 922 315265 🕐 Tue–Sun 9–7
(shorter hours in winter)
💷 Moderate (Sun free)

Museo de Historia de Tenerife

The Casa Lercaro on Calle San Agustín is a grandiose 16th-century colonial mansion, and is the ideal setting for this impressive treasurehouse of island history. The house itself deserves a visit, and anyone really wanting to get a vivid overview of Tenerife's story since the arrival of the Spanish should certainly stop by for a couple of hours at this excellent museum. The collections include historical maps and maritime exhibits, and displays that take the story right up to the present.

✉ Calle San Agustín 22 ☎ 922 825949 🕙 Tue–Sun 9–7 💷 Inexpensive

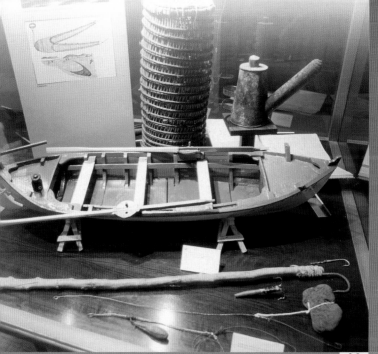

Plaza del Adelantado

The heart of old La Laguna is a pleasant, shaded square where locals relax on benches enclosed by some of the most striking historic and dignified buildings in town, including the Ayuntamiento (➤ 96) and the Santa Catalina church (➤ 98) – as well as beautiful mansions adorned with fine porches and balconies. There are bars here too, and the town's busy Mercado Municipal (main market), with its lattice gallery, is the place to join locals in the morning stocking up with fruit and vegetables.

✉ Mercado Municipal, Plaza del Adelantado ☎ 922 258774 🕐 Mon–Sat 8–1 🍴 *Tapas* bars around the square (€)

More to see in the North

BAJAMAR

One of the oldest resorts on Tenerife, Bajamar is a sharp contrast to the glitzier newcomers on the south coast. Here on the northern shores of the island, constant breezes and turbulent currents stir up the waves onto the black beach. For that reason bathers rarely venture into the sea. Instead, visitors do most of their swimming at the seashore lido and hotel pools. It's also a quieter, less crowded, less developed holiday environment – precisely what attracts its devotees. Once a fishing village, Bajamar (meaning 'down by the sea') has few signs of its past, with a long promenade and side turns, with many bars, restaurants and shops.

➕ 9A ✉ 15km (9 miles) northwest of La Laguna 🍴 Variety of bars and restaurants (€–€€) 🚌 105 (Santa Cruz–Bajamar) every 30 mins

CANDELARIA

The small and pleasant east-coast town of Candelaria makes a popular outing for locals, with its bars, pedestrianized main shopping street and its black beach. At one end of the town centre rises the large basilica, Nuestra Señora de la Candelaria, site of an important annual pilgrimage.

The Basilica of Our Lady of Candelaria is dedicated to the patron saint of the Canary Islands. Profoundly revered, she is always depicted holding the Child in her right arm and a candle in her left hand. Spiritually, her role is as the symbolic bringer of Christian light to the darkness of Guanche life, representing the rightness and justice of the Spanish occupation of the islands.

The legend told by early Spanish settlers – not by the Guanches – was that over a century before the arrival of the first Spanish *conquistadores* the Guanches found a statue of the Virgin and Child set up in a seaside cave. A multitude of legends claim the statue worked miracles to prevent the Guanches from harming her, and that the overawed Guanches began to worship the figure, which they called Chaxiraxi. In a mix of fact and fancy, it is related that the *mencey* (chieftain) of the Guanches welcomed the Spanish at this spot, but that the Guanches were already Christians when the conquerors arrived.

The huge **Basílica de Nuestra Señora de la Candelaria** (1958), set back from the sea, dominates the small town. Inside, the statue of the Virgin sits enthroned in a glorious gilt setting behind the altar, among devotional murals.

The statue dates from about 1830 – what became of the Guanches' Chaxiraxi (which may have looked quite different from

today's Virgin) is the stuff of
myth. Even before the Spanish
arrived in Tenerife, a European
living on Fuerteventura is said
to have stolen the Guanche
statue, but replaced it. Either
the original, or its copy, was
damaged by fire in 1789 and
repaired or replaced. That
statue was washed out to sea
and lost in 1826, being replaced
by the present version a few
years later.

Along the waterfront
esplanade stand sturdy,
dignified, sad statues,

representing the Guanche chiefs who ruled the island before the Spanish arrived.

✚ 9D ✉ On the coast 17km (10.5 miles) south of Santa Cruz 🍴 Bars and restaurants in the town centre (€–€€) 🚌 122, 123, 124, 127, 131 from Santa Cruz ❓ Festival of the Virgin of Candelaria 14–15 Aug (➤ 25)

Basílica de Nuestra Señora de la Candelaria

✉ Plaza de la Basílica, Candelaria 🕐 Daily 7:30–1, 3–7:30 ✋ Free

CASA DE CARTA, MUSEO DE ANTROPOLOGÍA

Best places to see, ➤ 50–51.

CASA DEL VINO LA BARANDA

Usually known simply as the Casa del Vino, this superb *bodega* (wine cellar) in a converted 17th-century farmhouse makes an enjoyable and educational outing – and a great excuse to stock up on local wine. A small payment enables visitors to taste any 10 of the 150 wines stocked here. Not simply a shop, it sets out to inform tourists about the range and qualities of Tenerife wines.

For those who want to go deeper into the subject, the building houses a small wine museum. It also shows a 10-minute film on the history of wine-making on the island, and explains why here, as in many other wine regions, quality has much improved in recent years. The restaurant (open to all) has panoramic views, as well as good food.

✚ 8B ✉ 1km (0.5 miles) from Autopista del Norte, at Km 21 (Exit 13, El Sauzal) ☎ 922 572535 🕐 Tue 11:30–7:30, Wed–Sat 10–10, Sun and public hols 11–6 (wine tastings until 10) ✋ Free 🍴 Restaurant on site (€€) ☎ 922 563388 🚌 101 Puerto de la Cruz–Santa Cruz; 012 from La Laguna

EL SAUZAL

This is a delightful community of attractive homes and pretty terraced gardens, and of particular interest is an unusual domed church in Moorish style, the Iglesia de San Pedro. El Sauzal's greatest attractions, however, are its wine museum (Casa del Vino la Baranda; ➤ opposite) and the exceptional coastal view, especially from the Mirador de la Garañona, which gazes along the sheer cliffs dropping into the sea.

A little further along the road, Tacoronte is the heart of Tenerife's wine-making area, noted for its *malvasia* (malmsey) vineyards and its two handsome churches.

✚ 8B ✉ About 16km (10 miles) north of Puerto de la Cruz
🍴 Many fish restaurants (€–€€) 🚌 101 every 30 mins
(Puerto de la Cruz–Santa Cruz); 012 from La Laguna

GÜÍMAR

On the border between the green north and the dry south, Güímar is an authentic Tenerife community that sees few tourists. Up the slope behind the town is the Ethnographic Park, the six curious large mounds of the enigmatic Tenerife step pyramids (➤ 54–55).

🞖 8E ✉ About 23km (14 miles) southwest of Santa Cruz, and 3km (2 miles) inland from the coastal highway 🍴 Bars and restaurants in the town (€) 🚌 120 from Santa Cruz every 30 mins ❓ Popular carnival first week Feb; ancient midsummer festival in Jun

HIDALGO, PUNTA DEL

If you want to stay at a Tenerife holiday resort yet get away from it all and remain far from the crowds, come to Punta del Hidalgo. Located at the end of a small road on the rocky Hidalgo headland that projects into the Atlantic from the northern coast, it's exposed to wild seas and strong winds. The resort does have its following – it's popular with German visitors and well known as a good place to enjoy the sunset. Its hotels give a fine view over the sea and the nearby Montañas de Anaga (➤ 110). Most visitors make little use of the sea, preferring to relax at hotel pools. Nevertheless, the resort is growing and gradually extending towards its similar neighbour, Bajamar (➤ 101).

🞖 9A ✉ 20km (12.5 miles) north of La Laguna

a drive in the Northern Hills

Allow a full day to explore the mountainous northern reaches of the island. This is the part which is paradoxically both the most and the least developed, with big working towns on the coast and in the valleys, simple hamlets scattered across the upper slopes, and breathtaking panoramic views from the hill crests. Begin the drive at Santa Cruz, or join at Tacoronte or at any point on the route if coming from the west or south.

Head north for 8km (5 miles) on the coastal highway (TF-11) to San Andrés and the Playa de las Teresitas (➤ 111). Turn inland for 10km (6 miles) on TF-12, the twisting, climbing road to Mirador El Bailadero.

You're now climbing into the Anaga Mountains (➤ 110). El Bailadero is a magnificent viewpoint, with sweeping vistas of mountain and coast.

Take the high cumbre (ridge or crest) road, TF-12, towards Mount Taborno. At the fork after 7km (4 miles), take the summit road.

A succession of views along this high road includes Mount Taborno's spectacular Mirador Pico del Inglés (a few metres up a side turn on the left) and Cruz del Carmen, where there is a 17th-century chapel and a restaurant.

After Las Mercedes turn right at Las Canteras on TF-13 to Tejina. At Tejina, follow TF-16 as it turns left towards Tacoronte. About 7km (4 miles) beyond Tejina, just before Valle de Guerra, pause at the Casa de Carta.

Casa de Carta houses the island's Anthropology Museum (➤ 50–51), a 17th-century farmhouse. Continue on this road to Tacoronte, the wine town (➤ 105).

Head east on the TF-5 to return to Santa Cruz.

Distance 90km (56 miles)
Time 4 hours
Start/end point Santa Cruz de Tenerife ✚ 10C
Lunch Mirador Cruz del Carmen (€€) north of La Laguna
🍴 Several in resorts (€–€€) 🚌 105 (Santa Cruz–Punta del Hidalgo) every 30 mins

LAS MONTAÑAS DE ANAGA

Tenerife's northern range of soaring, wild mountains remains remarkably unspoiled and is an ideal region for rambling and exploring well off the beaten track. Narrow, twisting roads give access to dramatic, rugged landscapes, while for walkers it is still possible to see villages that can be reached only by negotiating rough tracks. Here islanders lead a simple subsistence life, without any modern conveniences.

Long-distance paths have been waymarked by ICONA, the Spanish conservation agency. The ICONA signposting is clear, so you're not likely to get lost. However, it is unwise to walk without a detailed map. Walking maps can be obtained at the Puerto de la Cruz and Santa Cruz tourist offices and guided walks through the Anaga region can be organized. There is also an information centre at the Mirador Cruz del Carmen, where maps and pamphlets giving details of set walks are available. Wear good hiking boots and be prepared for changes in weather conditions.

Part of the region has been designated a protected area, the Parque Rural de Anaga. Yet though impressive and steep, the peaks are not high – Taborno, the highest point, reaches only 1,024m (3,360ft), and a road follows the crests, giving superb views from a string of *miradores*. However, the exposed northern terrain is often misty, wet or even lightly snow covered on winter days.

🔼 12A 📧 North of Santa Cruz 🍴 Mirador Cruz del Carmen (€€)
🚌 073, 075, 076, 077 from La Laguna

TERESITAS, PLAYA DE LAS

Despite its huge popularity, the appeal of Tenerife pre-dates the sun-sea-and-sand recipe of today's mass tourism. Most northern beaches are unattractive and consist of rough, dark volcanic material (a shock to some visitors). However, island authorities are aware of the lack and have created some artificial beaches.

By far the most outstanding of these is the beautiful curve of Playa de las Teresitas, created in the 1970s with sand from the Sahara desert. Ironically, it was created not in the tourist heartland of the south, but in the far north, where locals could enjoy it. San Andrés, at one end of the beach, is a working fishing village with a lively atmosphere.

➕ 11B ✉ San Andrés, 8km (5 miles) north of Santa Cruz 🍴 Bars and fish restaurants in San Andrés (€–€€) 🚌 910 from Santa Cruz; 246 (Santa Cruz–Almaciga) stops 3 or 4 times daily

HOTELS

GÜÍMAR
Finca Salamanca (€€)

This is a charming farmhouse in lush gardens, surrounded by avocado, mango and citrus groves. The rustic architecture sets off the stylish interior and arts and crafts, and a former barn is now an airy restaurant serving Canarian specialities and a selection of local wines.

✉ TF-61, Carretera Güímar, El Puertito km 1.5 ☎ 922 514530; 922 514531; www.hotel-fincasalamanca.com

LA LAGUNA
Nivaria (€)

In a town with few holiday hotels, the three-star Aparthotel Nivaria offers comfortable apartments and suites. The Nivaria has a bar/café, serves breakfast for guests and offers free internet. In the centre of the old district.

✉ 11 Plaza del Adelantado ☎ 922 264052; www.hotelnivaria.com

SANTA CRUZ DE TENERIFE
Atlántico (€)

This pleasant, Spanish-orientated hotel is located in the main shopping street at the heart of the city. Defined as a two-star, it is modest and adequately equipped.

✉ Calle Castillo 12 ☎ 922 246375

Contemporanéo (€€)

A modern three-star hotel almost free of English or German voices, located close to the Mencey, the García Sanabria park and the Rambla ring road. There's a restaurant and snack bar.

✉ Rambla General Franco 116 ☎ 922 271571; www.hotelcontemporaneo.com

Mencey (€€€)

Mencey is the name for a Guanche chieftain, and this elegant Sheraton hotel is chief among northern Tenerife's traditional five-star accommodation. In sumptuous colonial style with lavish

marble, fine woodwork and artworks, it offers every possible amenity in a peaceful location on the north side of the Ramblas.
✉ Avenida Doctor José Naveiras 38 ☎ 922 609900; www.sheraton.com

Pelinor (€)

A good example of a smaller hotel close to Plaza de España and aimed at Spanish visitors. It has comfortable rooms and a bar.
✉ Calle Béthencourt Alphonso 8 ☎ 922 246875; www.hotelpelinortenerife.com

Plaza (€€)

On an agreeable square in the city centre, close to shops, restaurants and entertainment, this comfortable hotel makes a good base.
✉ Plaza de la Candelaria 10 ☎ 922 272453

Taburiente (€€)

An aura of old-world grandeur clings to this long-established, classically furnished hotel. Many rooms have views over Parque Municipal García Sanabria and it's an easy walk to the main sights.
✉ Avenida Doctor José Naveiras 24A ☎ 922 276000

RESTAURANTS

CANDELARIA
El Archete (€€)

A smarter than usual restaurant, serving high-quality creative Canarian cooking. Something of a find in this region.
✉ Lomo de Aroba 2 ☎ 922 500354 🕐 Lunch, dinner; closed Tue pm—Wed

EL SAUZAL
Casa del Vino La Baranda (€€)

See page 60.

La Amistad (€–€€)

One the area's unpretentious restaurants, offering excellent Canarian and Spanish stews, roasts, fish and *papas arruagadas*.
✉ Calle Real Arotova (at Ravelo) ☎ 922 584299 🕐 Lunch, dinner; closed all day Wed and Sun eve

EL ROSARIO
Las Cañadas (€–€€)
Coloured lights and Canarian-style balconies set the tone for this popular restaurant. One of several jolly eateries in this farming area, it attracts local families for traditional roast meats, local wine and plenty of conversation and laughter.

✉ 71 General de la Esperanza ☎ 922 548030 🕔 Lunch, dinner; closed Thu

LA LAGUNA
Casa Maquila (€€)
La Laguna is not known for fine dining, but this simple, agreeable place is a good choice for local specialities, properly prepared.

✉ Callejón de Maquila 4 ☎ 922 257020 🕔 Lunch, dinner; closed Wed

Hoya del Camello (€€)
La Laguna's better restaurants are a short distance out of town, and this moderately priced *bodega* is one of them, with a menu of well-prepared international, Spanish and Canarian favourites.

✉ Carretera General del Norte 128 ☎ 922 262054 🕔 Lunch, dinner; closed early May, late Aug, Sun eve, Mon

Los Limoneros (€€€)
Rural but very civilized, this restaurant draws local families for big, well-prepared dinners and weekend feasts of international and local dishes, including rabbit in spicy sauce. The service is good.

✉ 447 Carretera General del Norte, Los Naranjeros, 4km (2.5 miles) east of Tacoronte ☎ 922 636637 🕔 Daily 1–11pm

SAN ANDRÉS
The cluster of humble restaurants (€–€€) along the waterfront of this pleasant little harbour village is well known to locals. The establishments all serve seafood at similar prices.

SANTA CRUZ
Café del Príncipe (€–€€)
Attractive, authentic and on one of the most appealing squares in Santa Cruz. Sit out with locals and tourists and enjoy a drink,

a snack or a complete meal of typical island specialities.

✉ Plaza del Príncipe de Asturias ☎ 922 278810 🕔 Tue–Sun 9–midnight

El Libano (€)

A long-standing favourite with locals, this Lebanese restaurant serves popular dishes of the eastern Mediterranean.

✉ Calle Santiago Cuadrado 36 ☎ 922 285914 🕔 Lunch, dinner

Le Bouchon (€€)

Genuine French cooking, and excellent French cheeses and wines, make this one of the best dining experiences on the island.

✉ Avenida Anaga 7 ☎ 922 031755 🕔 Mon–Fri 7:30am–11pm, Sat 9am–11pm, Sun breakfast and lunch; closed Tue

Los Troncos (€€)

See page 61.

TEGUESTE
Casa Tomás (€)

A simple, family-run restaurant offering home-style and authentic cooking. Wines are local, sometimes straight from the cask. *Costillas con papas* (cutlets with potatoes) is a typical dish.

✉ El Portezuelo ☎ 922 638007 🕔 Sep–Jul Tue–Sun noon–11pm; closed Mon

El Drago (€€€)

One of Tenerife's leading restaurants, this charming old farmhouse produces classic yet creative Canarian cooking; specialities include fish casseroles and rabbit in spicy sauce. There's a good wine list.

✉ Calle Marqués de Celada 2, El Socorro ☎ 922 543001 (reservations); www.mesoneldrago.com 🕔 Tue–Sun lunch, Fri–Sat dinner; closed Aug

SHOPPING

A range of locally made items can be found at the following craft stores. It may be worth shopping around, as the stock varies from place to place. Shop hours are generally Mon–Sat 9–1, 4–8.

Artenerife (Empresa Insular de Artesania)
Official chain offering guaranteed authentic, quality local crafts.
✉ Plaza de España, Santa Cruz ☎ 922 291523; www.artenerife.com

Mercado de Artesanía Española
A good choice of island handicrafts.
✉ Plaza de la Candelaria 8, Santa Cruz

HYPERMARKET SHOPPING
The Continente *centro comercial* has a huge hypermarket, and there are over 100 other shops on the site.
✉ 5km (3 miles) south of Santa Cruz by the Santa Maria del Mar exit of the Autopista del Sur ⏰ Mon–Sat 10–10

MARKETS
Mercado Nuestra Señora de África, Santa Cruz
Best places to see, ➤ 48–49.

Rastro
This big flea market takes place in streets around the Mercado.
✉ Calle José Manuel Guimerá, Santa Cruz ⏰ Sun 10–2

ENTERTAINMENT

Santa Cruz, not as touristy as southern resorts, has cheaper discos and late-night bars – look along Avenida Anaga and Rambla del General Franco. Don't miss the city's open-air discos during high summer. The scene tends to be quiet on weeknights.

ARTS AND DRAMA
Tenerife has several concert halls and theatres. Most of the island's culture is located in Santa Cruz and La Laguna.

SANTA CRUZ
Auditorio de Tenerife
Tenerife's excellent concert hall (➤ 80), designed by Spanish architect Santiago Calatrava, is home to the Orquesta Symphony Orchestra. It offers classical music, including *zarzuela* (Spanish

light opera), musicals, jazz, rock and world music, and is the venue of the annual Music Festival, the archipelago's leading classical music event (begins early January for 3–4 weeks).

✉ Avenida Constitución 1 ☎ 922 568600

Teatro Guimerá

Plays (in Spanish), opera and concerts. Most major concerts are now held at the Auditorio, but this charming theatre is still used for smaller musical events. See also page 81.

✉ Plaza Isla de la Madera ☎ 922 364603; 922 606923

LA LAGUNA

Little frequented by tourists, the town is Tenerife's centre of contemporary culture, and hosts the island's Jazz Festival and International Theatre Festival.

Teatro Leal

Hosts concerts, exhibitions and festival events.

✉ Calle Obispo Rey Redondo ☎ 922 601100

CASINO
Casino Santa Cruz

Roulette, blackjack and poker at Tenerife's poshest hotel. There's a formal dress code.

✉ Hotel Mencey, Avenida Doctor José Naveiras 38, Santa Cruz
☎ 922 290740 🕔 From 8pm

NIGHTLIFE
Santa Cruz

The people who jam into Santa Cruz's nightspots are mainly young Spanish visitors, and more adventurous foreign tourists. It's liveliest around Avenida Anaga between midnight and 5am, and in summer there are open-air discos. Plaza de la Paz is more sedate.

Nooctua

A perennially popular veteran among late-night venues.

✉ Autopista Norte, Carretera Guamasa ☎ 922 636999

SPORT

ADVENTURE SPORTS

El Cardon Educatión Ambiental

This company conducts scuba, sea kayaking, climbing, mountain bike and caving expeditions throughout the island. They also have a hostal and shop in the Teno Rural Park.

✉ Plaza Los Remedios 2, Buena Vista del Norte ☎ 922 127938; www.elcardon.com

GOLF

Many visitors come to Tenerife just to play on the excellent golf courses, four of which are between Playa de las Américas and Reina Sofía Airport.

El Peñon Club de Golf Tenerife

An 18-hole course founded in 1932 by British expatriates.

✉ Tacoronte, 14km (9 miles) from Santa Cruz ☎ 922 636607

Golf La Rosaleda

Laid out amid lush banana plantations and trees, with views to the Orotava Valley and Mont Teide, with nine par-3 holes.

✉ Camino Carrasco 13, Puerto de la Cruz ☎ 922 373000; www.golflarosaleda.es

WATER SPORTS

Scuba and offshore diving is popular all around the islands. Near-constant trade winds and warm, clean waters ensure ideal conditions for windsurfing and surfing around the south coast.

Barlovento

Canoeing, sailing, water-skiing, windsurfing and boat rental.

✉ Parque Marítimo César Manrique, Santa Cruz ☎ 922 223840

Centro Insular de Deportes Marinos (CIDEMAT)

Canoeing, diving, sailing, water-skiing and windsurfing.

✉ Carretera San Andrés-Valleseco, Santa Cruz ☎ 922 597 525; www.deportestenerife.com

The West

Puerto de
la Cruz

Parque Nacional
del Teide

If the island is divided into two, north and south, then most of western Tenerife belongs to the north – it is luxuriant, full of colour, life and history. Yet even so the west is different. Here, away from the busy valleys and towns of the northern peninsula, there is a sense of space and distance and a remoteness from Spain.

The climate is hotter and drier, the land more visibly volcanic, the atmosphere more serene. The ever-present feature is the pale summit of El Teide, rising above all else.

Tenerife's first tourists were drawn to Puerto de la Cruz, and smaller resorts formed to either side of it, clinging to the rocky shores, eventually turning the corner at the Macizo de Teno (Teno Massif) and heading down into the south. Those early holidaymakers belonged to a more refined age, and even today the western resorts retain a calmer, less unruly air and attract a more discerning crowd.

PUERTO DE LA CRUZ

Simply 'Puerto' to old hands, Puerto de la Cruz (Port of the Cross) was the first town on Tenerife to attract tourists – and for good reason. Ideally placed for both north and south, yet at a distance from the workaday world of Santa Cruz, this historic port has a lovely setting and was a perfect base for the leisurely, civilized sightseeing before the days of 'sun, sea and sand'.

Built in the 1600s by the settlers at La Orotava, Puerto grew into a major port after the 1706 eruption destroyed the harbour at Garachico. Blessed in every way, the town is green and luxuriant, with a delightful setting at the foot of steep slopes and with an exquisite climate. It clings to the seashore, backed by the lush Orotava Valley with Pico del Teide clearly visible beyond. Fortunate Puerto is a vibrant, living community that does not depend only on tourism. Its million visitors a year are among the island's most discerning tourists, and enhance the town's charming, bustling atmosphere. After the advent of mass tourism, the new crowds went south to purpose-built resorts, allowing old Puerto to keep its air of dignity. At the same time it has adapted to the changing needs of tourism, with numerous quality hotels, good shopping, sophisticated entertainment, a casino, pretty public spaces and some of the best family attractions on Tenerife.

✚ 6C 🛈 Plaza de Europa 5 ☎ 922 386000 ⏰ Mon–Fri 9–8, Sat–Sun 9–1

Bananera El Guanche

Bananera El Guanche is a popular family attraction devoted to the subject of the banana, a staple of the island economy with the majority taken by Spain (the Dwarf Cavendish variety cannot be exported due to EU regulations).

Entertaining and informative, Bananera is set in an old banana

plantation *(bananera)*, and a video (every 20 mins) explains the method of cultivation, a complicated and arduous process even though plants reproduce without pollination. The first banana plants were brought here some 500 years ago from Indo-China, en route to the newly discovered West Indies, then in 1855 the Dwarf Cavendish, or Chinese banana, was introduced, and consequently became especially associated with the Canary Islands.

Visitors stroll along a route through various kinds of banana and other plants, such as papaya, mango, the huge and ancient *drago* (or dragon tree), sugar cane, cotton, coffee, cocoa, peanuts, pineapples and more. There's a large cactus garden, a Tropical Plantation with a wide range of fruit trees and exotic flowers too, including the elegant bird of paradise flowers, which have become a symbol of the Canary Islands and a popular souvenir.

Finally, before leaving, you're offered a free taste of banana liqueur (powerful – and sweet) and a ripe banana.

✉ La Finca Tropical, 2km (1.2 miles) from Puerto de la Cruz on the road to La Orotava ☎ 922 330017 🕐 Daily 9–6 💷 Expensive 🍴 Bar on site (€), restaurants in town (€–€€€) 🚌 Free bus from Puerto de la Cruz 9:30–12:45 and 2:30–5:45, every 20 or 30 mins

Castillo de San Felipe

A sturdy little coastal fortification, the diminutive Castillo de San Felipe is named after King Philip IV of Spain (1621–65). It was during his reign that settlers began to construct Tenerife's first capital, La Orotava, and its port, Puerto de la Cruz. The Castillo dates from that period and it remains the best example in the Canary Islands of the Spanish colonial style of architecture. The building has been immaculately restored and is now a cultural centre. Classical concerts are often given here, which provide visitors with a pleasing change from the usual type of entertainment on offer. The castillo also houses art exhibitions.

✉ Paseo de Luis Lavagi
🕐 Open for events and exhibitions 🖐 Variable
🍴 In Calle de San Felipe
(€–€€)

Ermita de San Telmo

San Telmo (St Elmo) is the patron saint of sailors, and the seafarers of Puerto de la Cruz erected this simple waterfront chapel in his honour in 1626 (it was rebuilt in 1780 after a fire). Its also known as the Capilla de San Telmo (Chapel of St Elmo). Dazzling white, it stands in a lovely little garden surrounded by the noisy ebb and flow of tourists and traffic.

Although the street outside is named after the church, as is a nearby beach, there is something that touches the soul in this humble place. Here fishermen gave thanks for having been spared from the dangers of the ocean, while beneath the floor are buried some who were less fortunate, victims of a flood in 1826.

✉ Calle de San Telmo 🕐 Daily. Services Wed, Sat 6:30pm, Sun 9:30, 11am
✋ Free

Iglesia de Nuestra Señora de la Peña de Francia

Puerto's main church, the Church of Our Lady of the Rock of France, was started in the 1680s and took nearly 20 years to complete – even then it lacked the pale angular bell tower, added as an afterthought some 200 years later. Standing among the tall palms and flowering shrubs near the elegant swan-shaped central fountain in Plaza de la Iglesia, the church possesses a sombre dignity. The baroque interior is decorated with some fine statuary, as well as an ornate altarpiece by Luis de la Cruz in a side chapel. The organ comes from London, ordered and installed in 1814 by Bernardo de Cologán, one of several Canary islanders of Irish origin. Notice, too, the striking wooden pulpit, painted to look like marble.

✉ Calle la Hoya, Plaza de la Iglesia ☎ 922 380051 🕐 Mon–Sat 3–7, Sun 9–7. Mass daily 8:30, 6:30, 7. International Mass (usually in English) Sun at 10am ✋ Free 🍴 Drink or snack on the terrace of Hotel Marquesa, Calle Quintana 11 (€€)

Jardín Acuático Risco Bello

Looking up at the almost vertical hillside, it's hard to believe it could be home to a water garden, but this green Eden holds ponds, pools, grottoes, bridges, stone staircases and meandering walkways through gardens containing more than 600 plant varieties. Tucked into this profusion are benches, where guests can sit and relax while admiring the artistry of the landscaped scenery. The variety is amazing, from reeds and lilies to grape arbours and full-grown fig trees. Terraces and bridges provide different vantage points and perspectives on a thoroughly delightful garden. Tea is served on the lawn above.

✉ Carretera Taoro 15, Puerto de la Cruz 🕐 Daily 9:30–6
✋ Moderate 🍴 Tea, coffee, pastries (€)

Jardín Botánico

One of the most enjoyable places in Puerto is the exuberant, exotic and colourful Botanical Gardens on the edge of town. It's the perfect place to grab a cool moment of tranquillity. Here hundreds of intriguing plant varieties grow in profusion, set in a peaceful shady park of just 2.5ha (6 acres). In places, roots, branches and twisting trunks form a fascinating sculptural tangle. Almost everything in the gardens is native to some other land, the focal point being a huge 200-year-old fig tree, brought as a sapling from South America. Today it rears up on an astonishing platform of roots, an unarguable testimony to the benign climate and conditions here. The range of species, in several hundred varieties, is prodigious; some can also be seen at the Bananera El Guanche

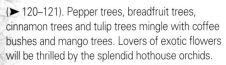

(▶ 120–121). Pepper trees, breadfruit trees, cinnamon trees and tulip trees mingle with coffee bushes and mango trees. Lovers of exotic flowers will be thrilled by the splendid hothouse orchids.

The gardens were set up in 1788 by King Carlos III as part of an experiment to see if plants from other climate zones could be acclimatized, and whether useful varieties growing in tropical colonies could be 'trained' to survive in Spain. The correct name of the Jardín Botánico to this day is El Jardín de Aclimatación de La Orotava (La Orotava Acclimatization Garden). Tropical plants that thrived here were then taken to gardens in Madrid and Aranjuez in Spain to see whether t hey could 'learn' to survive on the mainland, but it proved simply too cold in winter and the results were broadly unsuccessful. It is now better understood that while some plants can prosper away from home others cannot; for most of the exotics growing in the Jardín Botánico, Tenerife was as far as they were willing to travel.

✉ Calle Retama 2, off Carretera del Botánico
☎ 922 383572 ⏰ Summer daily 9–7; winter daily 9–6
✋ Inexpensive 🍴 Hotel Botánico (▶ 142–143); no casual dress 🚌 Along Carretera del Botánico

Lago Martiánez

As a traditional resort, Puerto de la Cruz had a major drawback in the new era of mass package tourism: it had no decent beach. The solution was this lido, now looking a little dated, designed by the inspirational architect César Manrique and completed in 1977. Manrique was also responsible for the town's Playa Jardín, which he developed in 1992 (➤ 128).

In the 1970s, when the town wondered how to respond to the growing demand for swimming and sunbathing facilities, it consulted Manrique, who was based on Lanzarote. An internationally acclaimed modern artist, he had recently returned to his native Canary Islands, where he had been given a free hand to develop tourist attractions.

Manrique had strong views on mass tourism, which he believed could be of great benefit to the Canary Islands, but at the same time risked destroying the landscape, local culture and traditional architecture. He argued that tourism should be encouraged within strict controls and that facilities should be of the highest, most creative standard.

Marketed under various names (Costa Martiánez, Lido de San Telmo, Lido de Martiánez), the Lago contains filtered seawater. It consists of attractively shaped swimming pools, interspersed with refreshing fountains and islets of lush greenery, and has proved a great success. Waterside sunbathing terraces, shaded by palms, are laid out around the main pool.

Touches of art and humour are everywhere: a popular feature is a central lava isle which periodically erupts as a fountain. The summit of El Teide makes a dramatic backdrop. Besides on-site bars and restaurants, there's also a glitzy cabaret show-restaurant called Andromeda.

✉ Playa Martiánez, Avenida de Colón ☎ 922 385955 ⏰ Oct–Apr daily 10–5; May–Sep 10–6 💲 Moderate 🍴 Eating places on site and nearby (€–€€€) 🚌 Along waterfront

Loro Parque

Best places to see, ➤ 44–45.

Museo Arqueológico

Near the old fishing harbour, this small archaeological museum is housed in an attractive 19th-century building. The collection relates to the ethnography of the Guanche people. Interesting permanent displays include early maps, ceramics, equipment used in farming, jewellery, weapons and information on mummification. The museum hosts temporary exhibitions.

✉ Calle del Lomo 9A ☎ 922 371465 🕔 Tue–Sat 10–1, 5–9, Sun 10–1
♿ Inexpensive (free Thu) 🍽 Eating places nearby (€), especially in Calle de San Felipe

Playa Jardín

In 1992, following his success with the Lago Martiánez (➤ 126) nearer the town centre, the Canarian artist César Manrique transformed the neglected rocky bay near the Castillo de San Felipe into a remarkable waterfront beach garden. The site was chosen partly because the coast is more sheltered here and has less dangerous currents. Tons of dark sand were imported to form a stretch of beach, with gardens of flowering bushes, palms and exotics cultivated on the surrounding sand and rock. Rocks rising inland add a backdrop to the scene.

Thousands of offshore concrete wave breakers hidden beneath the water protect Manrique's beach and gardens from the power of the ocean. As a result, despite its shortcomings, Playa Jardín has become become one of the resort's most popular beaches (➤ 59). It has been awarded a Blue Flag, a symbol of good environmental standards and safety.

✉ At the western end of town, near Punta Brava ✋ Free 🍴 In the nearby fishermen's quarter, especially Calle San Felipe (€–€€) 🚌 102, 325, 343, 381, 382 from the resort centre

Plaza del Charco

A *charco* is a pool or pond, and this animated raised square stands where once shallow waters collected from the sea and locals fished for shrimps. Now the plaza, with its ancient Indian laurel trees, is the very heart of Puerto's old quarter and full of life – with bars and cafés, buskers and strollers. The charming restored 18th-century Rincón del Puerto, on the west side, has traditional balconies and a courtyard, now occupied by bars.

✉ Off Calle Blanco, near the fishing harbour 🍴 Bars and restaurants in the square (€–€€)

Puerto Pesquero

There's no better reminder that Puerto does not exist only for tourists than this small working fishing harbour, not far from lively Plaza del Charco. A low harbour wall of black volcanic stone encloses the little bay. A few modest but brightly painted rowing boats are hauled up on the shore, where local men and boys gather to talk or work.

On one corner, beside the water, a handsome building is the former Casa de la Real Aduana – the Royal Customs House. Built in 1620, this small public office continued to function as a customs house until 1833 and is now is the new tourist information office. Behind are 18th-century harbour defences that protected the town and port from raiders.

Across the street, Casa de Miranda, which dates back to 1730, is a fine house that was once the home of Venezuelan liberator Francisco Miranda. It has been restored and is now home to a bar and restaurant (► 146).

✉ At the end of Calle Blanco 🍴 In Calle Blanco and Plaza del Charco (€–€€)
ℹ Tourist Information Office ☎ 922 388777

a walk around Puerto

Puerto still has an atmosphere of history and much of the central area of this attractive town is pedestrianized.

Start from Plaza de la Iglesia.

This handsome square, with its palms and a lovely swan fountain, is dominated by the church (➤ 123).

Take Calle de Cologán (away from the sea) and turn into the second right, Calle Iriarte.

Reaching Plaza Concejil and Calle San Juan, you'll find the elegant balconied 18th-century house Casa Iriarte to the right, now a souvenir shop. On your left is the landmark Palacio Ventosa, with its tall tower.

Continuing along Calle Iriarte, turn right into Calle Blanco.

This brings you to Plaza del Charco, the pleasantly bustling and shaded heart of town (➤ 128).

Take Calle de San Felipe from the northwest corner of the square.

This street has unpretentious restaurants and traditional Canarian buildings of character. Turn right and then right again into Calle de Lomo, for the Museo Arqueológico (➤ 127).

Retrace your steps to Plaza del Charco, then turn left on Calle Blanco towards the sea.

Here is the Puerto Pesquero (➤ 129), the endearing little

harbour with the modest Casa de la Real Aduana (Royal Customs House) on one corner.

Follow the main seashore road (Calle de Santo Domingo) eastwards past Punta del Viento (Windy Point), eventually reaching Calle de San Telmo.

Pause to admire the tiny Ermita de San Telmo (▶ 122–123). Continue to the Lago Martiánez (▶ 126).

Distance 1.5km (almost 1 mile)
Time 1.5 hours
Start point Plaza de Iglesia
End point Lago Martiánez
Lunch Bars and restaurants (€–€€) ✉ Plaza del Charco, Calle de San Felipe

More to see in the West

GARACHICO
Best places to see, ➤ 42–43.

ICOD DE LOS VINOS
A highlight of any tour around Tenerife is the little town of Icod. Its main attraction is the gigantic Dragon Tree known – with poetic licence – as the Drago Milenario, the Thousand-Year-Old Dragon Tree (➤ 38–39). But Icod has other charms too. The Plaza de la Iglesia has a lovely 15th-century church, the Iglesia de San Marcos, containing a baroque altarpiece, a fine timber ceiling and a magnificent cross from Cuba, a masterpiece of delicate silverwork.

Nearby, the Mariposario del Drago (Butterfly Garden) is a flutter with colourful tropical butterflies.

As the name suggests, Icod is also known for its wines. Taste and buy them at shops near Plaza de la Iglesia, such as Casa del Vino or Casa del Drago.

✚ 4D 🍴 Bars and restaurants 🚌 107, 108, 325 ⚡ Fiestas on 22 Jan, 25 Mar, 24 Jun and 29 Nov; Corpus Christi in Jun; Santa Barbara end Aug; Dragon Tree Festival in Sep ℹ Calle San Sebastian 6 ☎ 922 812123

MACIZO DE TENO (TENO MASSIF)

The volcanic basalt mountains are among the most ancient rocks of the island. Their unusual geology and flora, and the steep, buckled terrain make the Teno Massif a splendid place for hiking.

Masca, a mountain village perched above a deep gorge, was once remote and virtually inaccessible. Now a daringly engineered road has made it a popular excursion, with roadside restaurants providing dazzling views. Another improved road leads west from the little regional centre of Buenavista del Norte to Tenerife's most westerly point, the Punta de Teno, a dramatic headland with a lighthouse, where the Atlantic breaks against black rocks. Buenavista del Norte has a pretty main square with some 18th-century mansions; the church of Nuestra Señora de los Remedios has fine altarpieces and a notable *mudéjar* (Islamic-style) ceiling.

✚ 1D 🍴 Bars and restaurants in Buenavista del Norte

LA OROTAVA

Puerto de la Cruz was originally built as the port for older, grander La Orotava, a hilltown just inland whose coat of arms still declares it to be a Villa Muy Noble y Leal (most noble and loyal town). A jewelbox of balconied facades, pretty decoration, stone-paved streets and preserved historic buildings, La Orotava is best explored on foot. Start with the wonderful views from Plaza de la Constitución. The towers and dome of baroque Iglesia de Nuestra Señora de la Concepción in Plaza Casañas are a distinctive landmark.

Calle San Francisco is the highlight, climbing the west side of town from Plaza San Francisco to Plaza Casañas. Casa de los Balcones (➤ 36–37) is its main attraction. Across the street the **Casa del Turista,** though less grand, is older (c1590), and its craft shop offers demonstrations of making sand pictures, a feature of the town's Corpus Christi celebrations. Also along here, the 17th-century Hospital de la Santísima Trinidad used to be a convent – the revolving drum set in the wall by the main door was used to leave unwanted babies.

Interesting museums in town include **Museo de Artesanía Iberoamericana,** celebrating the artistic and cultural links between Spain

(including the Canary Islands) and Latin America; **Artenerife,** or **Casa Torrehermosa** (➤ 148), showcasing the best of the island's arts and crafts; and out-of-town **Museo de Cerámica,** with 1,000 pieces of traditional pottery.

✚ 7D ✉ 6km (4 miles) southeast of Puerto de la Cruz

🍴 Plaza de la Constitución 🚍 101, 107, 108, 345, 348, 350, 352 from Puerto de la Cruz

🛈 Carrera Escultor Estévez 2 ☎ 922 323041

Casa del Turista

✉ Calle San Francisco 4 ☎ 922 330629 🕒 Mon–Fri 8:30–6:30, Sat 8:30–5 ✋ Free

Museo de Artesanía Iberoamericana

✉ Calle Tomás Zerolo 34 ☎ 922 321746 🕒 Mon 9–3, Wed–Thu 9–5, Sat 9–1 ✋ Moderate

Artenerife or Casa Torrehermosa

✉ Calle Tomás Zerolo 27 ☎ 922 322285 🕒 Mon–Fri 9:30–6:30, Sat 9:30–2 ✋ Free

Museo de Cerámica

✉ 4km (2.5 miles) west of town centre at Calle León 3 ☎ 922 321447 🕒 Mon–Sat 10–6, Sun 10–2 ✋ Inexpensive

LOS GIGANTES

Best places to see, ➤ 46–47.

around western Tenerife

This day out takes in all the grandeur of Tenerife's volcanic heartland.

Leave Puerto de la Cruz, exiting at the junction for Tacoronte on the TF-5 heading towards Santa Cruz, (Tacoronte) for La Esperanza.

La Esperanza is popular for walks in the pine woods of the Bosque de la Esperanza, south on TF-24, the Carretera Dorsal, along the 'spine' of the island (► 139–140).

Take TF-24 south from La Esperanza. The road rises through pine woods, often shrouded in clouds or mist.

At a bend, a sign points the way to Las Raíces monument, marking the spot where General Franco met army officers to plan their coup. Viewpoints such as the Mirador Pico de las Flores offer dramatic views of the north coast. Eventually the road passes the observatory at Izaña and enters the national park (► 138–140).

Follow TF-24 to the junction with TF-21 and follow it to the left, continuing south.

The Centro de Visitantes
(➤ 139), at El Portillo pass,
marks the entrance to the
Caldera de las Cañadas.
After 11km (7 miles) of
volcanic terrain you reach
the El Teide cable car or
teleférico (➤ 139) and
4km (2.5 miles) further, the
parador, nearly opposite Los
Roques de García (➤ 142).

*At Boca del Tauce, the
typical Cañadas scenery
ends abruptly. Return
through the park to the
Centro de Visitantes at
El Portillo.*

Beyond El Portillo, take the
left-hand fork (TF-21) down
into the Valle de la Orotava,
passing through heath, vines
and, on the lowest level,
banana trees.

*Continue the descent into
Puerto de la Cruz.*

Distance 145km (90 miles)
Time 4 hours
Start/end point Puerto de la Cruz
➕ 6C
Lunch Restaurants near
El Portillo and the *parador*

PARQUE NACIONAL DEL TEIDE

The Guanche name for El Teide, the immense volcano rising at the heart of the island, was 'Tener Ife'. For them, the mountain was the island, though in geological terms that's only partly correct. It was the emergence of this volcano, along with the Anaga and Teno ranges, that created Tenerife and subsequently shaped the island's terrain and dominated its natural and cultural development.

While the northern fringes of the island are fertile and inhabited, the landscape around El Teide (➤ 40–41) remains harsh and unyielding. In particular, the area within the Caldera de las Cañadas, the remnants of a far bigger volcano whose eroded walls enclose El Teide, is an awesome combination of rock and dust. In 1954 the surroundings of El Teide were made a national park, its boundaries roughly following the borders of the caldera. Covering

189sq km (73sq miles), the whole park lies above 2,000m (6,560ft). It is strictly protected from any development. The park can be visited by car, by coach (on through road TF-21), by bicycle or on foot on numerous smaller tracks and paths. A cable car *(teleférico)* runs up El Teide to a point 163m (535ft) below the summit (➤ 41).

The **visitor centre** at the high El Portillo pass, east of El Teide on the park through road, provides an introduction to the national park. An exhibition and video explains the volcanoes and there is a garden of local flora. For walkers detailed maps of the park are available and excellent free guided walks set out from here (reserve a place by telephoning at least a day ahead). The *parador* too has a small visitor centre.

Teide National Park is a good choice for movie buffs. Intended to convey a primeval wilderness, it has featured in *The Ten Commandments* and *Planet of the Apes*. In the film *One Million Years BC* Raquel Welch appeared here wearing only a fur bikini.

➕ 16H 🚫 Always accessible 💵 Free 🍽 Restaurants (€€) at the visitor centre at El Portillo or the *parador* 🚌 348 leaves Puerto de la Cruz once a day at 9:15, arriving at the *parador* at 11:30; return trip at 4. The 342 leaves Playa de las Américas once a day at 9:15 and arrives at El Portillo at 11:45; return trip at 3:15 ❓ You can stay in the park at the Parador de Cañadas del Teide (☎ 922 374841)

Centro de Visitantes

✉ El Portillo ☎ 922 356000 🚫 Daily 9–4 💵 Free

Cumbre Dorsal

Of all the routes to the Teide National Park, the most spectacular is the Carretera Dorsal road (TF-24), along the crest of the Cumbre Dorsal – the uplands that run northeast from the national park to the Anaga Mountains. Their slopes rise behind the Orotava Valley,

with wonderful views to the sides and ahead. Along the road a number of *miradores* make unmissable stopping points (► 136–137).

➕ 7D

Las Cañadas

This spectacular caldera, a crater zone measuring some 16km (10 miles) across, consists of lava fields, sandy plateaux *(cañadas)* and several freakish natural phenomena. One in particular, Los Roques de García, comprises a majestic cluster of misshapen rocks, easily spotted just opposite the *parador*. A waymarked walk goes round the Roques and across a swirly lava flow. To the north looms the awesome peak of El Teide itself (► 40–41), while to the south lies the arid, sandy plain known as the Llano de Ucanca.

Another impressive rock formation is Los Azulejos (by the roadside about 1km/0.5 miles south of Los Roques de García). This geological curiosity takes its name from the brilliant blue-green colourations of the rocks (*azulejos* is Andalucian for glazed tiles), caused by deposits of iron and copper mineral salts.

➕ 16J ✉ Near TF-21 just south of the parador ✋ Free 🍽 The visitor cente at El Portillo has a choice of bars and restaurants (€–€€€) 🚌 348 once daily each way from Puerto de la Cruz to the *parador*; 342 once daily stops here from Playa de las Américas ❓ Choose clear, calm weather and come early to avoid the crowds

Paisaje Lunar (Lunar Landscape)

Accessible only on foot, this area of the park is a bizarre visual phenomenon. Here, high in the middle of nowhere, strange columns and shapes of tufa make a weird unearthly landscape. To reach the Lunar Landscape area involves an 11km (7-mile) round trip on marked footpaths just east of the *parador*.

➕ 16J

HOTELS

EL TANQUE
Caserío Los Partidos (€)
This charming little place lies tucked in the hilly terrain of Tenerife's northwest corner, with views towards Pico del Teide. Each bedroom is individually designed with an open fireplace and immaculate bathroom. Terraces and courtyards bright with flowers and fountains spill around the building. *Tapas* are on the evening menu. This retreat is a long way from the congested coastal resorts and appeals primarily to walkers and visitors who value peace and quiet. A car is essential for exploring.
✉ Los Partidos 4, El Tanque-San José de los Llanos ☎ 922 693090; www.caserio-lospartidos.com

GARACHICO
Quinta Roja (€€)
A 16th-century country mansion, which escaped damage during the 1706 volcanic eruption, this handsome building retains its historic features while also being a tasteful, elegant and very comfortable modern hotel. A programme of activities is on offer, and guests can borrow mountain bikes.
✉ Glorieta de San Francisco ☎ 922 133377; www.quintaroja.com

San Roque (€€€)
One of the most unusual and delightful hotels on the island, this historic building stands in the middle of the waterfront. The place has an exquisite low-key elegance. Armchairs and potted plants are dotted about, and there's a lovely arcaded and balconied courtyard within. There are 20 well-equipped rooms. Excellent food is served by the courtyard pool.
✉ Calle Esteban de Ponte 32 ☎ 922 133435; www.hotelsanroque.com

LA OROTAVA
Victoria (€€)
This 17th-century Canarian mansion in the old quarter has been restored in period style to become a delightful traditional small hotel. The excellent glass-roofed restaurant is one of its most

attractive features, and is open to non-residents as well as hotel guests. A rooftop terrace commands views across the valley towards the sea.

✉ Calle Hermano Apolinar 8 ☎ 922 331683; www.hotelruralvictoria.com

LOS GIGANTES/PUERTO DE SANTIAGO
Barcelo Santiago (€€)

A popular, large (yet low-rise) hotel featured by several tour operators, this well-managed complex offers two pools, floodlit tennis courts, a restaurant, bars, evening entertainment and other facilities. The accommodation, in blocks around the pool area, consists of neat and adequate rooms.

✉ La Hondura 8, Puerto de Santiago ☎ 922 100912

PARQUE NACIONAL DEL TEIDE (TEIDE NATIONAL PARK)
Parador de las Cañadas del Teide (€€€)

Tenerife's only *parador* occupies a stunning location near the foot of El Teide and makes an exceptional touring and walking base. The hotel merges unobtrusively into the surrounding scene and picture windows overlook an array of weirdly eroded rocks. Inside, the hotel is comfortably cheerful, with exposed stonework and open fires to ward off the chill of the altitude. Spacious and well-equipped bedrooms. Excellent restaurant.

✉ Las Cañadas del Teide National Park ☎ 922 374841; www.parador.es

PUERTO DE LA CRUZ
Acuario

This small, quiet hotel sits on the hillside about a 25-minute walk from the waterfront. Rooms are small but clean and it has a beautiful rooftop pool and sun chairs. Internet available; parking behind the hotel.

✉ Parque de las Flores 36 ☎ 922 374142; www.acuariohotel.com

Botánico (€€€)

This is an exceptional five-star hotel, a member of the Leading Hotels of the World group, that's oozing relaxed elegance and offers the height of luxury and every modern facility. On the northeast side of town, it is quite a long way from the centre and from the sea.

✉ Avenida Richard Yeoward 1, Urbanización Botánico ☎ 922 381400; www.hotelbotanico.com

Dania Park Hotel (€€)

Consisting of sister hotels facing each other across the enticingly named Calle Cupido (Cupid Street), set well back from the sea and also a few minutes' walk from the heart of town, these long-established, mid-range hotels near the bus station include two restaurants, plenty of entertainment, rooftop pools and a nude sunbathing area. Guests can use the facilities of either hotel.

✉ Calle Cupido 11 ☎ 922 384040; www.daniamagec.com

Monopol (€€)

One of the town's earliest hotels, down by the waterfront in the historic quarter. Though much modernized, including the installation of a swimming pool, it has preserved many original features and retains a pleasing colonial feel, with cane furnishings and greenery on a charming patio.

✉ Calle Quintana 15 ☎ 922 384611

Semiramis (€€€)

This ambitious five-star hotel, up the coast from Playa Martiánez, is some distance from the centre of town but has lovely sea views from some rooms and offers every modern comfort.

✉ Leopoldo Cólogan Zulueta 12 ☎ 922 373200

Tigaiga (€€–€€€)

In the gorgeous garden setting of the Taoro Park area, above the town, this conventional tourist hotel has won awards for its environmental management. Unremarkable but comfortable, rooms have partial sea views and face either the Taoro Park or Pico del Teide. The pool area has a view over Puerto and there's a separate terrace for sunbathing.

✉ Parque Taoro 28 ☎ 922 383500; www.tigaiga.com

RESTAURANTS

BUENAVISTA DEL NORTE
Restaurante Mesón del Norte (€)
Enjoy the friendly atmosphere and traditional Canarian cooking at a reasonable price at Las Portelas in the Parque Rural de Teno area in the far west of the island.

✉ Las Portelas ☎ 922 128049 🕐 Lunch, dinner

GARACHICO
El Caleton (€–€€)
Perfectly located by the crashing waves on the waterfront facing the Castillo de San Miguel, this down-to-earth restaurant prepares good meat and fish dishes in Canarian or international style, or you can just stop by for a soup, snack or ice cream.

✉ Avenida Tomé Cano 1 ☎ 922 133301 🕐 Lunch, dinner

LA OROTAVA
Casa Egon (€)
Settle down to a glass or two with tasty *tapas* or a light meal of traditional Spanish and Canarian cooking at this popular, unpretentious and inexpensive bar-restaurant.

✉ Calle Leon 5 ☎ 922 330087 🕐 Closed Sun pm and all day Mon

Sabor Canario (€€)
Set in a fine, late 16th-century building, this charming restaurant is attached to the Museo del Pueblo Guanche in the heart of the old town – a showcase for Canarian crafts and food products. The restaurant serves authentic local dishes – try braised rabbit, roast cheeses or *ropa vieja* (literally 'old clothes', a classic Canarian hotpot). Head for a table in the plant-filled courtyard.

✉ Calle Carrera17–23 ☎ 922 322793 🕐 Mon–Sat lunch, dinner

Restaurant Victoria (€€)
Inside the striking Hotel Victoria is this courtyard restaurant, arguably the best in town, with a short menu of accomplished dishes inspired by local tradition. Very reasonably priced.

✉ Calle Hermano Apolinar 8 ☎ 922 331683 🕐 Tue–Sat 1–4:30, 8–11:30

LOS GIGANTES/PUERTO DE SANTIAGO
Casa Pancho (€€)
This authentic restaurant comes as a surprise in a popular sun-and-sea resort area, catering mainly for British people on package holidays and with few signs of any indigenous local life. There's nowhere else quite as good for some distance around as this genuine Spanish restaurant serving tasty food to a high standard.

✉ Playa de la Arena ☎ 922 861323 🕐 Jul–May Tue–Sat lunch, dinner

🚌 473 (Los Gigantes–Las Galletas, south of Los Cristianos)

Miranda (€€)
Imaginative local and international cuisine in the heart of Los Gigantes. Light, modern décor and a good range of steaks, seafood and Canarian wines.

✉ Calle Flor de Pascua 25 ☎ 922 860207 🕐 Dinner

LOS REALEJOS
El Monasterio (€€)
See page 60.

PARQUE NACIONAL DEL TEIDE (TEIDE NATIONAL PARK – INCLUDING BOUNDARY AREA)
El Portillo de la Villa (€–€€)
By the National Park Visitor Centre, this large house at the El Portillo junction near the slope of the volcano has a choice of restaurants serving simple snacks and meals.

✉ On the main road TF-21 at El Portillo, near junction with TF-24

☎ 922 356000 🕐 Daily 9–4

Restaurante Las Estrellas (€€)
Outside the village of Chío, on the southwest side of the national park boundary, this bar-restaurant has stirring coastal views.

✉ Carretera Boca-Tauce 21, Guia de Isora ☎ 922 850906 🕐 All day

🚌 460 (Icod–Guía de Isora, via Chío) every 2–3 hours

Parador de las Cañadas del Teide (€€)
See page 61.

PUERTO DE LA CRUZ

Casa de Miranda (€€)

This traditional Canarian house near Puerto's harbour square traces its ancestry back to 1730. A cheerful *tapas* bar decked with gingham tablecloths, red chilli peppers and hams occupies the ground floor; upstairs its galleried, plant-filled restaurant makes a romantic setting for Canarian and international fare all at reasonable prices.

✉ Plaza de Europa ☎ 922 373871 🕐 Lunch, dinner

Casa Regulo (€€–€€€)

A smart, solidly reliable high-quality restaurant near the old fishing harbour, serving beautifully prepared Canarian and international dishes, with especially good seafood. Good service and seating in a lovely courtyard.

✉ Calle Perez Zamora 16 ☎ 922 384506 🕐 Closed Sun, Mon lunch and Jul

Casino Taoro (€€€)

Puerto's casino is in Parque Taoro, the park set back from and above the bustle of the town. The casino restaurant attracts a dressed-up crowd and caters for them in style, with red-draped tables, formal service, smart atmosphere and a predictable range of classy international dishes. Good views.

✉ Casino, Parque Taoro ☎ 922 372660 🕐 Dinner

La Casona (€–€€)

Cook your own steak on a slab of hot stone at La Casona, one of the best of several Canarian/international eating choices in Rincón del Puerto, a handsome historic mansion and courtyard in Puerto's main square.

✉ 13–14 Plaza del Charco ☎ 922 373422 🕐 Lunch, dinner

La Papa (€€)

This is a small friendly restaurant in the old town center that specializes in local food prepared in the Canarian style.

✉ Calle San Felipe 33 ☎ 922 381663 🕐 Sun–Fri 12–3, 6–10

La Parilla (€€€)

A smart restaurant located in one of Tenerife's most luxurious hotels open to the public. It offers top international and French-style cooking, and slick service in an elegant setting. Dress is smart-casual.

✉ Hotel Botánico, Avenida Richard J Yeoward 1 ☎ 922 381400
🕒 Dinner

Lago Martiánez (€–€€€)

A couple of seafront restaurants provide snacks, drinks and complete meals in this pool complex (➤ 126).

✉ Avenida Colón ☎ 922 381752 🕒 Daily 10–5, then Andromeda open until late

Magnolia (€€€)

Top-class dining, indoors or alfresco, at this award-winning restaurant attracts discerning locals and well-to-do Spanish visitors. Food is a mix of Catalan and international, with the emphasis on fish and seafood. You'll find the restaurant out of town in the La Paz *urbanización*.

✉ Avenida del Marqués de Villanueva del Prado ☎ 922 385614 🕒 Dinner

Mario (€€–€€€)

This is one of a choice of eating establishments in the fine old Rincón de Puerto building. It specializes in skilfully prepared fish and seafood dishes.

✉ 12–14 Plaza del Charco ☎ 922 385535 🕒 Lunch, dinner

Palatino (€€–€€€)

An excellent range of seafood is served at this established and well-regarded restaurant in an elegant setting near the old fishing harbour.

✉ Calle del Lomo 28 ☎ 922 382378 🕒 Mon–Sat lunch, dinner; closed Jul

SHOPPING

HANDICRAFTS AND SOUVENIRS

Artenerife (Empresa Insular de Artesania)

Official chain of shops selling the finest genuine local handicrafts, including pottery, woodcarving, embroidery and lace. The Artenerife symbol is a guarantee of quality and authenticity.

✉ Casa Torrehermosa, Calle Tomás Zerolo 27, La Orotava ☎ 922 322285
✉ Waterfront, near Calle Esquina Mequinez, Puerto de la Cruz ☎ 922 378103 ✉ Casa de la Aduana, Calle de la Lonjas, Puerto de la Cruz ☎ 922 387103; www.artenerife.com

Casa de los Balcones

This beautifully restored 17th-century mansion (➤ 36–37 and 68) contains a craft shop where local people can often be seen at work. As well as inexpensive souvenirs, a wide range of quality items, such as Spanish and Canarian lace and linen and traditional embroideries, are on sale. Some are made on the premises, as the Casa de los Balcones also serves as a highly regarded school of embroidery.

✉ Calle San Francisco 3, La Orotava ☎ 922 330629;
www.casa-balcones.com

Casa del Turista

Located opposite La Orotava's famous Casa de los Balcones (➤ 36–37), this craft and souvenir shop has the same owners and stocks similar products.

✉ Calle San Francisco 4, La Orotava

Casa Iriarte

The disorganized store in this historic building has a selection of imported table linen.

✉ Calle San Juan 17, Puerto de la Cruz

MARKETS

Mercado Municipal San Felipe

✉ Avenida de Blas Pérez Gonzáles, Puerto de la Cruz 🕙 Mon–Sat am

ENTERTAINMENT

In Puerto de la Cruz, the nightlife is focused mainly on Avenida de Colón and its side streets. The scene is relaxed, good-humoured and civilized, with a number of bars offering live music and discos.

CASINOS
Casino Taoro

Tenerife's grandest casino is housed in a former hotel that played host to Europe's nobility over a century ago (➤ 80). Although badly damaged by fire in 1929, its lavish architecture and wonderful location high in the Parque Taoro guaranteed its survival, and it eventually reopened as a casino, offering slot machines as well as roulette and other gaming tables. There is a restaurant, and the casino is famous for its Cocktail Taoro, a fizzy and extravagant mix of champagne, calvados and banana liqueur served with lemon and caviar.

✉ Parque Taoro, Puerto de la Cruz ☎ 922 380550 🕓 From 8pm
🖐 Moderate ❓ Formal dress code; you must bring your passport

PUBS, CLUBS AND DISCOS
Caballo Blanco

Live local bands provide the music for dancing at this seafront venue with bars and a restaraunt.

✉ Hotel San Telmo, San Telmo 18, Puerto de la Cruz ☎ 922 385656

Café de Paris

There's music and dancing in the evenings at this café and bar close to the seafront

✉ Avenida Colón 2, Puerto de la Cruz ☎ 922 384000

Molly Malone

Home from home for the Irish, and a lot of fun for everyone else, at this lively pub near the harbour. There's the latest sport on TV and live music, including owner Des serenading with Irish songs, while the Guinness and Irish whiskey flow till the early hours.

✉ Calle Las Lonjas, Puerto de la Cruz ☎ 922 386164;
www.themollymalone.es

SHOWS
Andromeda
This popular, stylish cabaret and show restaurant was created by artist César Manriquez and is located at the Lago Martiánez on the seafront. It attracts world-class artistes and highly professional dancers and showgirls.

✉ Isla del Lago, Lago Martiánez, Puerto de la Cruz ☎ 922 383852

🕐 Dinner 8pm, floor show 10pm

Tenerife Palace
Start the evening with a complimentary cocktail and enjoy the 'tropical' music. A show with international artists starts at 9:15pm. See also page 81.

✉ Camino del Coche, Puerto de la Cruz ☎ 922 382960

SPORT

WRESTLING
One of the traditional island sports, called *la lucha* or *lucha canaria*, descended from pre-Spanish times, is a curious form of wrestling. With its own weekly TV show and frequent matches – which send usually restrained Canarios wild with excitement – Canarian wrestling has become very popular. Two teams compete by pitting one man against another, in turns, until there is a clear victory. The men, wearing a particular style of shorts and shirt, try to throw each other to the ground by gripping the side of each other's clothing. It is slow and careful, with sudden moves as they try to catch each other off guard. Tourists are welcome to matches; ask at hotels or the tourist office for details and venues. Demonstrations of *lucha canaria* are given at the Hotel Tigaiga:

✉ Hotel Tigaiga, Parque Taoro 28, Puerto de la Cruz ☎ 922 383500

🕐 Sun 11am

The South

The climate that caused Spanish colonists to stay in the green north of the island is the very thing that has caused foreign tourists to flock to the south. Everything beyond the volcanic lands around El Teide is bone dry, a land stripped bare by Saharan sun. The light is dazzlingly pure and clear, the hills casting magical views across the emptiness to a perfect blue sea.

For centuries this was the least valuable part of the island, in places little more than a desert. Up on the slopes some simple, remote shepherd villages survived, while down on the coast the harbour of Los Cristianos benefited from its sheltered position out of the wind. Now, though, the south is full of life and entertainment. Today that once-empty southern coast harvests Tenerife's most valuable crop: sun-seeking tourists. And for them, there can be no better place to be on this island.

COSTA ADEJE, LOS CRISTIANOS AND
PLAYA DE LAS AMÉRICAS

These three very different resorts, merging into one another on the southern tip of the island, are the heart of Tenerife's package holiday country. Chances are you have chosen to stay here – and for sun, sea and sand, it's the right choice. Taken together, they offer a huge choice of accommodation, as well as round-the-clock bars with satellite TV, scores of restaurants and entertainment for all tastes. The centre of the action is Playa de las Américas. To its east is Los Cristianos, with a busy harbour and excellent beach, while on the west side is the newer, classier Costa Adeje.

➕ 14L: Costa Adeje and Playa de las Américas; 15L: Los Cristianos ✉ Exits 27, 28, 29 or 30 of Autopista del Sur 🍴 Tourist restaurants (€–€€€) near beaches and close to Puerto Colón and Los Cristianos harbour 🚌 111 to Santa Cruz. Frequent services to all southern resorts; collect timetable from any tourist office. For TITSA bus information ☎ 922 531300

Aqualand

A hugely popular waterpark with pools, rides, slides, flumes, wild water and dolphin displays. Many families, especially those with younger children, prefer to base themselves here throughout their stay.
✉ Exit 29 of Autopista del Sur ☎ 922 715266; www.aqualand.es 🕐 Daily 10–6 ✋ Expensive 🍴 On site (€–€€) 🚌 Free from southern resorts

Costa Adeje

Extending north from Playa de las Américas, this vast development runs to La Caleta and beyond. Aiming upmarket, many of its newer hotels are elegant and imaginative with masses of marble, lush gardens and state-of-the-art facilities. Included in the area are Playa Fañabé and the smaller Playa del Duque. Puerto Colón, a smart marina of ocean-going yachts, is a real focal point in this area.

🛈 Playa de Troya, Avenida Rafael Puig 1, Adeje ☎ 922 750633

🛈 Playa Fañabé, Avenida Litoral, Adeje ☎ 922 716539 🕓 Mon–Fri 9–5
(4pm Jul–Sep)

Jardines del Atlántico Bananera

Though overshadowed by Bananera in Puerto de la Cruz (▶ 120–
121), this one offers an opportunity to see, taste and learn about
bananas on a genuine banana farm. You'll also learn other things
about Tenerife, including crops and wild plants, and how El Teide
distributes the rainwater. There are guided tours of the gardens.
✉ Exit 26 of Autopista del Sur ☎ 922 720403 🕓 Mon–Fri 10–6 (last
admission 4:15), closed Sat–Sun 🚻 Expensive 🍽 On site (€€) 🚌 Free from
southern resorts

Los Cristianos

This was the only coastal town already in existence in the late 1960s, when sun-seekers arrived in the south. It already had a few bars and a good natural beach, and owed its existence as a port to a location well sheltered from the wind. Even with the subsequent massive growth, the town maintains its identity, and away from the seafront there's a refreshing sense of reality often lacking at the newer resort next door. On the other hand, Los Cristianos now has a slightly dated air, and some of the accommodation and amenities look poor. The focal point is the bustling harbour, from where ferries go to La Gomera.

🛈 Centro Cultural (Casa de la Cultura) Plaza del Pescador 1 ☎ 922 757137 🕐 Mon–Fri 9–3:30, Sat 9–1 ⛴ Hydrofoil and ferry services to La Gomera. Boat trips from the harbour

Parque Las Aguilas – Jungle Park

This park is a great alternative to the beach for kids. Bird shows are the highlight, and condors, flamingos, pelicans and penguins are among the creatures living here. There are also crocodiles, pygmy hippos and tigers, and rare breeds such as white lions. This is a really unusual zoo, with tree-top climbs and a chance to feed animals in their cages, plus various rides and other amusements (➤ 70–71).

www.aguilasjunglepark.com

✉ By junction 27, Autopista Sur, near Los Cristianos ☎ 922 729010 🕐 Daily 10–5:30, last admission 4:30

👋 Expensive 🍴 On site (€€) 🚌 Free from resorts

Playa de las Américas

Playa de las Américas is unfocused, sprawling, low budget, and much of it is unattractive, but it rightly remains supremely popular. It has successfully upgraded, investment in its beaches has improved the quality of the sand, and it's perfect for those who want to start the day at noon with a full English breakfast, tan all afternoon, and disco dance all night.

🛈 Avenida Rafael Puig 19 ☎ 922 797668 🕔 Mon–Fri 9–9, Sat–Sun 9–3:30
🚢 Boat excursions from Puerto Colón

Playa del Camisón

This lovely sheltered bay of soft sand, backed by a tree-lined walkway, is backed by the Mare Nostrum Resort (► 58 and 166). There's an enjoyable beach restaurant at one end.

✉ Between Playa de las Americás and Los Cristianos

More to see in the South

ADEJE

One of the few places in the south with a natural water supply, this appealing, unspoiled little southern hilltown has a stunning setting close to dramatic, jagged mountains. It makes an enjoyable short outing from the coast and is the starting point for walks to the Barranco del Infierno (➤ 158–159). It was once a Guanche tribal settlement and later became the Tenerife base of the counts of Gomera, who had plantations here worked by 1,000 African slaves. Ruins of the counts' fortress, Casa Fuerte, can be seen, and there's a 16th-century church, Iglesia de Santa Ursula.

✚ 15K ✉ 6km (4 miles) north from Playa de las Américas
🍴 Otelo (➤ 167) 🚌 416 (Granadilla–Guia de Isora) and 416, 473, 477 (Los Cristianos– La Caleta) run via Playa de las Américas to Adeje every 30 mins

COSTA DEL SILENCIO

This budget resort area was one of the first tourist developments, though its name has become rather incongruous since the construction here of Reina Sofía Airport. There are almost no proper beaches – just the odd shingle strip. Costa del Silencio includes Las Galletas, with two small beaches and a waterfront promenade, and Ten-Bel, one of Tenerife's first purpose-built, self-catering resorts.

✚ 16M ✉ 8km (5 miles) from Exit 26 of Autopista del Sur
🍴 Las Galletas waterfront has bars and restaurants (€–€€)
🚌 470 serves all towns from Las Americas to Playa Médano. Others serve specific towns

EL MÉDANO

This water sports resort on the island's exposed southeast corner has the best natural beaches, but is generally too windy for sunbathing to be enjoyable. There's a wind farm on the hills nearby. International windsurfing contests are held here, and anyone who really enjoys the sport should visit. The resort itself, on the headland of Punta del Médano, lacks charm and is very close to the international airport.

✠ 17L ✉ Exit 22 of Autopista del Sur, 22km (13.5 miles) from Los Cristianos 🍴 Bars and restaurants on waterfront (€–€€) 🚌 470 and other buses (Playa de las Américas–El Médano) ℹ Plaza de los Príncipes de España ☎ 922 176002 🕓 Mon–Fri 9–2/3, Sat 9–1

around the Barranco del Infierno

This excellent walk is much easier than the hike up El Teide (➤ 40–41). It's on a good path with few weather problems and no risk of altitude sickness. To protect the environment, entrance to the path is limited to 200 per day (with no more than 80 people at any one time), and you must book at least a day ahead. The Barranco del Infierno is the valley of a stream that rises on the southeastern slopes of the Teide National Park (over 2,000m/6,560ft above sea level). This walk covers the short stretch above Adeje, where a

**stream flows through a dramatic canyon, the
deepest in the Canary Islands. Wear sturdy shoes,
start early to avoid crowds and the heat (carry
water).**

*Start at Adeje (▶ 156). Take the road that runs uphill
through its centre. Continue on the steep road that leads
to the gorge path.*

At the entrance to the gorge, get a ticket at the Natural
Reserve booth. The path is fairly flat. Notice the caves high
in the rock face – Guanche mummies were found in them.
The scenery is dramatic. The stream, at first in a concrete
gulley, is the only permanent watercourse in the south. In
places vegetation is lush. Further on, the gorge narrows.

*The path crosses and re-crosses
the stream, now no longer
flowing through a gully.*

There are some steep sections, but
the total altitude gain is only 300m
(984ft). Finally the path arrives at La
Cascada, a waterfall in three levels
pouring into a natural pool, where it
is pleasant to rest and swim.

Return along the same path.

Distance 8km (5 miles)
Time 3–4 hours.
🚶 Entrance fee: €3 (book ahead on
☎ 922 782885)
Start/end point Adeje ✚ 15K
Lunch Otelo (▶ 167) ✉ At the gorge
entrance, overlooking the village

LOS ABRIGOS

A former fishing village close to Reina Sofía Airport, Los Abrigos is noted for its waterfront fish restaurants and has two beaches. Behind the village lies the Golf del Sur golf course.

✚ 16L ✉ 3km (2 miles) from Exit 24 of Autopista del Sur ▐▌ Along Paseo Marítimo (€–€€)

PARQUES EXÓTICOS

An astonishing sight in the midst of so much barren terrain, this lush tropical garden to the east of Los Cristianos is truly exotic. The main attraction is Amazonia, a slice of tropical rain forest created inside a climatically controlled domed area; it's suitably hot and muggy inside, and parrots, hummingbirds and some 5,000 butterflies fly freely around. Other attractions include a reptile house, a well-stocked cactus garden and a zoo park. Many of the

animals have been chosen with children in mind and include friendly marmosets and squirrel-monkeys. Visitors can even go inside the cages.

➕ 15L ✉ Exit 26 of Autopista del Sur, 3km (2 miles) northeast of Los Cristianos ☎ 922 795424 🕐 Daily 10–6 (7 in summer) 🖐 Expensive 🍴 Restaurant on site (€€) 🚌 Free hourly shuttle bus from Playa de las Américas and Los Cristianos

VILAFLOR

Quite unlike other settlements in the south, the prettily named 'flower town' is the highest village in the Canary Islands. Standing at 1,160m (3,806ft), it rises through cultivated terraces to a pine forest on the volcanic slopes of the Teide National Park. The vineyards of Vilaflor produce drinkable dry white wines, and the village also has an abundant natural spring, from which the water is bottled and sold all over the island. Although millions pass through Vilaflor on their way to the national park, few pause here and it consequently remains unspoiled. On the village outskirts are a couple of *artesanía* centres, which are useful places to buy local arts and crafts.

Just outside the village, set back from the main road, the little chapel called the Ermita de San Roque stands by the viewpoint Mirador de San Roque. From here there is a majestic panorama across southern Tenerife down to the dazzling coast.

➕ 16K ✉ On C821, 23km (14 miles) northeast of Los Cristianos 🍴 El Sombrerito (€€), Santa Catalina 🚌 342 from Playa de las Américas; 342, 382 from Los Cristianos

a drive in the south

Leave the resorts behind, climbing into near-barren, sun-baked landscapes.

From Los Cristanos take the Arona road, TF-665 (changes to TF-28 after the Autopista junction).

Pass through the village of Valle de San Lorenzo to reach Mirador de la Centinela for a sweeping view over a landscape of volcanic cones.

About 2km (1 mile) further on, minor road TF-565 turns left towards Vilaflor. It climbs steeply, eventually reaching the TF-51 at Escalona, where you turn right to continue climbing. The road skirts Montaña del Pozo (1,294m/4,245ft).

Along here walled vineyard terraces climb the slopes to Vilaflor (➤ 161), the highest village in the Canary Islands, noted for its white wines.

On reaching Vilaflor, turn left onto the TF-21 and keep climbing.

Above the village, past the Ermita de San Roque, pause at the Mirador de San Roque for a tremendous view. Almost at once the road enters the fragrant pine forest that encircles Las Cañadas (➤ 140). A twisting mountain road through the forest gives more good *mirador* views as Pico del Teide comes into view.

The road leaves the forest and at Boca del Tauce enters the volcanic Caldera de las Cañadas (➤ 138–139). Take a left onto the TF-38 for Chío.

The road cuts across a dark landscape of cones and lava flows. Eventually you reach the pine forests once more. There's a pleasant picnic site and rest area *(zona recreativa)* near Chío. The road descends sharply. Before Chío there are good views down to the sea, with La Gomera visible across the water.

At the Chío junction turn left and left again onto the TF-82. Pass unspoiled little Guía de Isora. Cross a succession of barrancos (gorges), eventually reaching the Autopista del Sur (TF-1). Take Exit 27 or 28 for Los Cristianos.

Distance 106km (66 miles)
Time 3 hours driving
Start/end point Los Cristianos ✚ 15L
Lunch stop Las Estrellas (€€) ✉ Just before Chío

HOTELS

ADEJE
Fonda Central (€)

On the main street of this beautifully located hill village close to the coast, this is a lovely little hotel run by a likeable couple. It provides good, simple accommodation and a garden restaurant offering local and international dishes.

✉ Calle Grande 26 ☎ 922 781550; www.fondacentral.es

COSTA ADEJE
Colón Guanahani (€€€)

An attractive low-rise building in neoclassical style, with marble and columns and arches. Pathways wander among shrubs and palms, and the heated seawater pool is ringed by trees. There's a good restaurant, plenty of facilities, entertainment and kid's club.

✉ Calle Bruselas, Playa de Fañabé ☎ 922 712046; www.colonguanahani.com

Gran Hotel Bahía del Duque (€€€)

One of Tenerife's most extravagant hotels, on a large secluded plot at the northern end of the resort, consists of 20 stylish buildings. The eyecatching lobby has aviaries, fountains, exotic flowers and murals and accommodation is in turretted blocks in the beautiful grounds. There's a choice of restaurants and an immaculate beach with an adventurous selection of water sports.

✉ Calle Alcalde Walter Paetzmann s/n ☎ 922 746900; www.bahia-duque.com

Iberostar Grand Hotel Anthelia Park (€€€)

This grandiose modern resort complex close to the beach consists of six small blocks catering for different types of guest – one for families, one quiet, one of luxury suites, and so on. All rooms have a sea view and there are plenty of amenities and services, such as five pools, three restaurants, several bars, a kindergarten, a night club and, more unusually, a library.

✉ Calle de Londres 15, Playa del Duque ☎ 922 713335; www.iberostar.com

Jardín Tropical (€€€)

Not far from Puerto Colón, this is a superb, award-winning resort hotel. Its imaginative white Moorish style, beautiful pool area, lush vegetation and seafront location add up to a wonderful place to stay. There are five restaurants in the hotel.

✉ Calle Gran Bretaña ☎ 922 746000; www.jardin-tropical.com

Jardines de Nivaria (€€€)

In the quieter, western end of the resort, at Playa de Fañabé, this hotel incorporates local themes into its architecture. There is a pool area and one of the seawater pools is heated in winter.

✉ Calle Paris ☎ 922 713333; www.nivaria.es

GOLF DEL SUR
Vincci Tenerife Golf (€€)

The seafront hotel stands near Reina Sofía Airport, 100m (110yds) from the golf course. The air-conditioned rooms all have a balcony and are equipped with cable TV. There's a buffet restaurant, a seawater pool (heated in winter), tennis court and entertainment.

✉ Urb. Golf del Sur San Miguel ☎ 922 717337; www.vinccihotels.com

LA ESCALONA
Finca Vista Bonita

Finca Vista Bonita lives up to its name, a set of 13 generously sized apartments set in the midst of farming country with balconies overlooking sea and mountains. Gardens, pool, free internet and satellite TV.

✉ Calle el Portillo, San Miguel de Abona ☎ 922 712 928; www.finca-vistabonita.com 🚌 TITSA bus 116, 416

LOS CRISTIANOS
Tenerife Sur Apartments (€€)

This pleasing aparthotel, offering comfortable and attractive suites of moderate size, is about four blocks from the beach. There's a good pool area, sauna, restaurant, snack bar, and supermarket.

✉ Calle Amsterdam 3, off Avenida de los Cristianos ☎ 922 791478

PLAYA DEL CAMISÓN
Mare Nostrum Resort (€€)

On a large beachfront plot, this resort, with a grandiose 'ancient world' theme of classical fountains and statues, comprises five hotels with a total of more than 1,000 rooms, including 100 suites with private pools. Guests can use the facilities – which are extensive – of any hotel (except the exclusive Sir Anthony), and the complex includes the Pirámide de Arona, with Tenerife's largest theatre and one of its best restaurants.

✉ Avenida de las Américas ☎ 922 757545; www.expogrupo.com

PLAYA DE LAS AMÉRICAS
Bitácora (€€)

One of the big popular holiday hotels, the Bitácora is very comfortable and well equipped. It has a large swimming pool surrounded by spacious lawns and plenty of other attractions and facilities for families. Generous buffets.

✉ Avenida Antonio Domíguez Alfonso 1 ☎ 922 787740; www.springhoteles.com

Las Dalias (€€)

The huge and popular Las Dalias, with 800 beds, offers a poolside terrace, paella at the afternoon barbecue and a nightly disco. Nearby Los Hibiscos, Bougainville Playa and Torviscas Playa hotels are similar and belong to the same group, with central reservations.

✉ Calle Gran Bretaña ☎ 922 792712; www.iberostar.com

Tenerife Best (€€€)

The Tenerife Best is a very attractive, popular hotel that achieves a high standard. The hotel is located in beautiful landscaped grounds with a swimming pool and waterfall area. There is a very good choice of food and a varied programme of entertainments is laid on.

✉ Avenida Antonio Domínguez Alfonso 6 ☎ 922 792751

RESTAURANTS

ADEJE
Las Rocas (€€€)
See page 61.

Otelo (€)
Get a drink or a good meal at this modest, likeable bar-restaurant, brilliantly situated near the entrance to the Barranco del Infierno. Well known to expatriates and old Tenerife hands, it's especially popular for the island's traditional rabbit dishes, spicy chicken and Canarian specialities. Hearty portions and a pleasant atmosphere.
✉ Molinos 44, Villa de Adeje ☎ 922 780374 🕐 Wed–Mon 10am–midnight

EL MÉDANO
Avencio (€)
This reliable, inexpensive seafront favourite offers a cosy interior of rustic and nautical décor. Fresh seafood is always a safe bet, but there's plenty else on the menu. Catalan and Rioja wines accompany local vintages.
✉ Calle Chasna 6 ☎ 922 176079 🕐 Oct–Aug Tue–Sun; closed Sun dinner

EL TANQUE
Monte Verde (€€)
Located at a development further up the coast from El Médano, this restaurant offers a range of international, Spanish and Canarian cuisine that includes first-rate steaks. There are tables set up outside, and a children's play area.
✉ Avenida Príncipes de España 2, El Tanque ☎ 922 136502
🕐 Lunch, dinner

LOS ABRIGOS
La Langostera (€–€€)
See page 60.

Perlas del Mar e Hijos (€€)
Of all the fish restaurants lining the water's edge at Los Abrigos, this one has perhaps the best location, just above the waterline.

Select your fish from the counter and specify how you want it cooked (steamed, grilled, fried). Terrace tables make a fine spot to watch the sun set over the waves and the planes landing and taking off from Reina Sofía Airport.

✉ Paseo Maritimo ☎ 922 170014 🕐 Lunch, dinner

LOS CRISTIANOS
Arepera Gomerón (€)

Offering budget-priced unpretentious cooking, this functional restaurant by the bus station specializes in tasty Canarian fish and steak dishes.

✉ Avenida Juan Carlos 1 ☎ 922 751377 🕐 Lunch, dinner

La Cava (€€)
See page 60.

Papa Luigi (€–€€)

A cosy Italian restaurant in the town centre, decorated with terracotta pots and gingham table-cloths. The menu presents an extensive range of familiar variations on the themes of pasta and pizza, in addition to a selection of fish and meat dishes. Cooking is more than competent and the service is courteously efficient.

✉ Avenida Suecia 40 ☎ 922 750911 🕐 Lunch, dinner

PLAYA DEL CAMISÓN
La Pirámide (€€€)

Broad steps lead up to the spectacular La Pirámide, a spacious restaurant decorated in red, blue and white, with large chandeliers, a grand piano and efficient service. Best of all are opera nights – Tuesday, Friday and Saturday (8:30–11), when four young opera singers stand among the diners and perform.

✉ Avenida de las Américas ☎ 922 796360 🕐 Dinner

PLAYA DE LAS AMÉRICAS/COSTA ADEJE

There are dozens of inexpensive bar-restaurants near the waterfront, with basic meals of pasta, pizza, paella, steak, fish and chips and other favourites displayed in photos on boards outside.

El Molino Blanco (€–€€€)

Though aimed mainly at foreign tourists, the rustic setting and welcoming atmosphere of the white windmill are enjoyable. Dining areas spill on to shady flower-filled terraces. The menu and wine list are wide-ranging, with unusual items like goat or ostrich.

✉ Avenida de Austria 5 ☎ 922 796282 ⏰ Wed–Mon 1pm–1am

El Patio (€€€)

Among the very best dining experiences on the south coast. Enjoy a high-quality Canarian and Spanish meal on the terrace of this hotel-restaurant near the Puerto Colón.

✉ Jardín Tropical Hotel, Calle Gran Bretaña ☎ 922 746061; www.jardin-tropical.com ⏰ Dinner Tue–Sat 7–11

La Hacienda (€€–€€€)

One of the elegant restaurants in the luxury hotel complex of the Bahía del Duque (▶ 164). Dress up for a memorable treat.

✉ Gran Hotel Bahía del Duque, Playa del Duque ☎ 922 746900; www.bahia-duque.com ⏰ Lunch, dinner

Mamma Rosa (€€€)

This very popular restaurant demands a certain smartness from diners to match the good food, fine wine and professional service.

✉ Apartamentos Colón, Avenida Santiago Puig ☎ 922 794819; www.mammarosa.com ⏰ Lunch, dinner

Wolfi (€)

An attractive terrace with expansive sea views is the setting for a range of good snacks and meals.

✉ Calle Eugenio Dominguez Alfonso ☎ 922 790927 ⏰ All day and evening

PORIS DE ABONA
Casablanca (€€)

From the motorway (Porís exit) track down this roomy restaurant near the seafront. Cuisine includes paella and home-made cheese, there's an interesting house wine, and often live folk music.

✉ Carretera General ☎ 922 164296 ⏰ Tue–Sun lunch, dinner

SAN ISIDRO
El Jable (€€)
In this untouristy inland village near the motorway, close to the El Médano exit, there's an appealing and popular bar-restaurant serving hearty Canarian cooking.

✉ Calle Bentejui 9 ☎ 922 390698 ⏰ Tue–Sat 1–4, 7:30–11; closed Sun–Mon lunch 🚌 111 (Playa de las Américas–Santa Cruz)

SHOPPING

SHOPPING CENTRES
The best fashion, electrical and photographic shops and other boutiques are in attractive modern malls and purpose built complexes, such as Plaza del Duque (Costa Adeje), CC Gala and department store Maya (Playa del Camisón). The scruffy 'tax-free' and 'discount' bazaars close to the beachfronts are best avoided.

SOUVENIR AND CRAFT MARKETS
Tourist street markets take place in the resorts on certain days. Try the Torviscas beach area near Puerto Colón on Thursdays and Saturdays (9–2) and Los Abrigos on Tuesday evenings (6–10).

Casa de los Balcones
For more authentic, better-quality craft work visit the Gran Hotel Bahía del Duque (➤ 164). On the fifth floor of this luxury Costa Adeje hotel there's a sales outlet of the Casa de los Balcones.
⏰ Mon–Sat 9:30–4, 5:30–9:30

ENTERTAINMENT

PUBS, CLUBS AND DISCOS
Los Cristianos/Playa de las Américas
Las Veronicas, on the seafront road in Playa de las Américas, is the focal point for clubs and dance bars. Things liven up around 11pm, bars close 3am–6am. Here are a few of the popular venues:

Bobby's
Rated one of Playa's top dance clubs; gets going very late.
✉ Centro Comercial Veronicas, Playa de las Américas

Busby's
Right next door to Bobby's and sharing the same crowd.
✉ Centro Comercial Veronicas, Playa de las Américas

Caledonian Bar (The Cally)
Terrific young atmosphere and music at this disco pub; very mixed clientele but lots of Scots.
✉ Centro Comercial Starco, Playa de las Américas

Linekers Bar
Booze, telly, bar food and music and dance prevails at this noisy popular laddish sports pub opposite Las Veronicas.
✉ Centro Comercial Starco, Playa de las Américas

Rags
In the area known as The Patch, near Las Veronicas, this dance bar plays a mix of pop, R&B and party music.
✉ Centro Comercial, Playa de las Américas

Tramps
A very, very popular disco – but it closes periodically so call to check before setting out.
✉ Centro Comercial Veronicas, Playa de las Américas ☎ 922 790371

CABARET AND SHOWS
Pirámide de Arona
One of the largest and best theatres on the island stages a top-quality musical every evening. Changed annually, it is co-written by leading Spanish choreographer Carmen Mota and is always an exceptionally impressive and enjoyable show. See also page 80.
✉ Mare Nostrum Resort, Avenida de las Américas, Playa de las Américas
☎ 922 757549

Tropicana
For a good dinner and spectacular musical show and cabaret, visit Tropicana on Tuesday, Thursday, Saturday or Sunday evenings
✉ Autopista del Sur (Junction 79), Costa Adeje; www.tropicanatenerife.com

THEME DINNERS
Castillo San Miguel
You can pretend it's the Middle Ages in this mock-medieval castle. Dine in jolly mood to the accompaniment of tournaments and boisterous family fun with music, singing and dancing. See also page 80.

✉ Aldea Blanca, San Miguel, Autopista del Sur, junction 24
☎ 922 700276

SPORT

GOLF
Amarilla Golf
An 18-hole course beside coastal cliffs.

✉ Urbanización Amarilla Golf, San Miguel de Abona ☎ 922 730319;
www.amarillagolf.com

Centro de Golf Los Palos
A par-27 nine-hole course, just 6km (4 miles) east of Playa de las Américas. Small but plenty of challenges.

✉ Carretera Guaza–Las Galletas Km 7, Arona ☎ 922 169080;
www.golflospalos.com

Costa Adeje Golf
This fine 27-hole course has greens with several doglegs. Located 5km (3 miles) from Playa de las Américas, with views of La Gomera.

✉ Finca de los Olivos, Adeje ☎ 922 710000; www.golfcostaadeje.com

Golf del Sur
This 27-hole course has hosted several major international events.

✉ Urbanización Golf del Sur, San Miguel de Abona ☎ 922 738170;
www.golfdelsur.net

Golf Las Américas
A 72-par course just outside Playa de las Américas and Los Cristianos; 18 holes.

✉ Exit 28 of Autopista del Sur ☎ 922 752005; www.golf-tenerife.com

La Gomera

Despite efforts to attract visitors, the tiny island of La Gomera has so far escaped the onslaught of mass tourism. A wild green landscape of plunging *barrancos* has made development difficult, just as it made colonization impossible in centuries past. A new airport in the south may bring more people, but a lack of suitable facilities (though it does have two of the best hotels in the Canaries) ensures that La Gomera appeals mainly to those who need no entertaining, and want only to experience the simplicity and sun-warmed tranquillity of island life.

Yet La Gomera offers walks, ancient woodland and a dramatic history. The island's capital, San Sebastián, is easily accessible by ferries crossing the 32km (20 miles) from southern Tenerife. Even for those who feel they must be back at their Tenerife hotel in time for dinner, La Gomera makes a most memorable day out.

AGULO

A pearl of a village in a delightful setting above the coast, Agulo is enclosed by a semicircle of steep green hills, pouring with waterfalls and rushing streams after rain showers. The town's narrow cobbled streets are focused on a domed church with a Moorish appearance, while out to sea the inspiring vision of El Teide rises above the clouds that hang over the dark floating form that is the island of Tenerife. It's one of the prettiest spots on the north coast.

✚ *La Gomera 3b* ✉ 27km (17 miles) from San Sebastián on the northern road 🍴 Las Rosas (➤ 185–186) in Las Rosas hamlet, 2km (1 mile) west
❓ Fiesta of San Marcos 25 Apr; Los Piques mid- to late Jun (*silbo* language)

CHIPUDE

Until recently Chipude was a remote hamlet, lost high in the green heart of the island. While better roads and communications have changed all that, the villagers thankfully still preserve their old customs and traditions, and it is here that you may hear *silbo* – not being demonstrated for tourists, but used to call to friends or neighbours. Of all the distinctive elements in Canarian culture, few are more astonishing than the 'whistling language' of La Gomera. In response to similar conditions that gave rise to yodelling in Switzerland – needing to communicate across steep terrain and dense forests – the Gomerans developed a whole vocabulary, syntax and grammar of whistles. Another quality of *el silbo gomero* is its volume: skilled *silbadores* can whistle a detailed message that can be heard by another person up to 4km (2.5 miles) away.

Chipude has long been noted for its handmade pots made without a potter's wheel and decorated with traditional Guanche motifs, though in fact these are more often from the neighbouring village of El Cercado. In the surrounding area are other small, barely accessible rustic villages, including Pavón and Temocodá, also known for their fine handmade pots.

Legend has it that the extraordinary rock formation known as La Fortaleza, or the Chipude Fort, 2km (1 mile) south of the village, was a Guanche sacred site. This is easy to believe – its sheer stone soars vertically more than 1,200m (3,937ft) to a tabletop crest.

✚ *La Gomera 2d* ✉ 29km (18 miles) west from San Sebastián, off the central highland routes 🍴 Village bars (€)

HERMIGUA

Lying in the island's most fertile and productive valley, Hermigua tacks along the road through plantations of banana palms. Though one of La Gomera's larger settlements, it's a tiny, tranquil place, a

stopping point for visitors who want to see local handicrafts being made and make a purchase at the interesting Artesanía Los Telares. There is also a similar *artesanía* at Agulo, 3km (2miles) away. Nearly opposite Artesanía Los Telares is the Convento de Santo Domingo, a 16th-century church with a Moorish-style wooden ceiling.

✚ *La Gomera 3c* ✉ 20km (12.5 miles) from San Sebastián on the northern road 🍴 El Silbo (➤ 185), a simple bar-restaurant in the village 🚌 2, San Sebastian to Vallehermoso via Hermigua

LOS ÓRGANOS

Inaccessible from the land, these strange slender columns of basalt emerging from the sea to the northwest of Puerto de Vallehermoso are so named because they resemble organ pipes.

Extending over a 200m (656ft) stretch of cliff, and rising as much as 80m (262ft) from the sea, the tightly packed hexagonal columns make an impressive sight, and they certainly provide a good excuse for a boat excursion. Surprisingly, they do look just like the pipes of some gigantesque organ.

➕ *La Gomera 2b* ✉ 52km (32 miles) from San Sebastián on north coast 🍴 Bars in Vallehermoso (€) 🛥 Only accessible by boat, either from Puerto de Vallehermoso (4km/2.5 miles from Los Órganos), or on longer excursions from Playa de Santiago, Vueltas or San Sebastián

PARQUE NACIONAL DE GARAJONAY

While the sun beats down on the southern shore, a cooler, damper climate prevails around Mount Garajonay. Heather, ferns and lichens flourish, creating a thick carpet across the boulders and rocky slopes where the last of the native Canarian laurel woodland survives. Waterfalls and streams splash through the greenery. Walking in this wet, magical terrain among the slender, sinuous limbs of the Canary laurel *(Larus canariensis)*, it is certainly not hard to believe that you are in the Canary Islands. Not just laurel but also the luxuriant Canary date palm *(Phoenix canariensis)* grows here in great numbers, and there are over 400 species of native flowers, some found only at this place. There are also many insects and birds.

A useful starting point is the Centro de Visitantes (Visitor Centre) at Juego de Bolas, on the north side of the forest. This gives an overview of the park and its flora and fauna, has details of walks, and features demonstrations of such traditional skills as weaving, pottery, basketry and carpentry.

✚ *La Gomera 2c* ✉ Centro de Visitantes, Juego de Bolas, 35km (22 miles) from San Sebastián ☎ 922 800993 🕐 Tue–Sun 9:30–4:30. The craft workshops are open Tue–Fri only ✋ Free 🍽 Restaurants at La Laguna Grande (€–€€)

PLAYA DE SANTIAGO

The southernmost point of La Gomera, close to the island's airport, is blessed with a sheltered position, pebble beaches and an attractive setting. A growing success as a resort area, it was traditionally a large and prosperous fishing and farming village that went into decline in the 1970s. It has been reborn thanks to new water sports, beach and harbour facilities and the building of the impressive and imaginative upmarket resort hotel Jardín Tecina (➤ 185) by cruise operators Fred Olsen. The old

waterfront village is steadily expanding with the influx of bars and restaurants. At one end, a small fishermen's chapel decorated with model boats is set into the rock face.

✚ *La Gomera 3e*

✉ 30km (18.5 miles) southwest of San Sebastián 🍽 Simple restaurants on the waterfront (€–€€), Jardín Tecina hotel (➤ 185) ℹ Edificio Las Vistas, Local 8, Avenida Marítima s/n ☎ 922 895650

a drive in northern Gomera

The deeply cut, forested terrain of La Gomera restricts access, and until recently most journeys were made by boat, around the island's coast.

Start from San Sebastián on the Hermigua road, TF-711.

The road climbs up the Barranco del Cedro, passing a large statue of Christ that overlooks San Sebastián.

The road climbs higher and skirts the edges of the Parque Nacional de Garajonay.

Here the road winds through unspoiled woodland.

After sharp turns and a tunnel, the road begins descending towards the north coast.

Lovely views of green valleys and the blue ocean open up as the road descends to Hermigua (➤ 175) and Agulo (➤ 174).

The winding road climbs inland beside a plunging green valley and continues to Vallehermoso.

At Tamargada, pause at a fine *mirador* to view the forest. At Vallehermoso (➤ 184) there is abundant cultivation of date palms and bananas.

A poor road leads down to the shore at Puerto de Vallehermoso.

From the harbour, regular boat trips go out to see the strange rock formations of Los Órganos (➤ 176).

Distance 50km (31 miles)
Time 2–3 hours
Start point San Sebastián de la Gomera
✚ *La Gomera 4d*
End point Puerto de Vallehermoso
✚ *La Gomera 2b*
Lunch Las Rosas (➤ 185–186), or Tambur bar-restaurant (€) at the Juego de Bolas Visitor Centre

SAN SEBASTIÁN DE LA GOMERA

La Gomera's capital, usually known as San Sebastián and often known to locals simply as Villa, is an unprepossessing little port, though it has an excellent harbour. In several ways San Sebastián is quite untypical of the island. Though hemmed in by hills, the town lies on flat ground while the rest of La Gomera is all steep slopes and valleys; its dusty, dry setting is a marked contrast to the island's exotic greenery. Most of the town is modern white cubes in an island full of rustic character. Only San Sebastián's picturesque main street, Calle Real (sometimes known as Calle

del Medio), and the main square, Plaza de las Américas, with its balconied mansions, evoke the memory of colonial times and the great drama of the island's history.

La Gomera was the last Canary Island to be subjugated by the Spanish – it remained independent until 1837. As a result, no other Canary Island retains so much of the native Guanche culture and ethnicity. There are, too, visible in many island faces, reminders of the many African slaves who were kept here.

When Christopher Columbus anchored at San Sebastián before the voyage that discovered the Americas, this was the most westerly port in the world. Tenerife remained in Guanche hands, while on La Gomera only this edge of the island was under Spanish control.

To recapture a little of that past, walk along the main street, Calle Real. Here is the 17th-century Casa del Pozo, once the customs house; the name means House of the Well. Inside is the **Pozo de la Aguada,** the well from which Columbus's quartermaster drew the water to supply his ships on the outward voyage to America. Here too the expedition bought seeds, grains and flowers to be planted in the New World.

In the same street stands the **Iglesia Nuestra Señora de la Asunción** (Church of Our Lady of the Assumption), where – we are told, but this is poetic licence – Columbus said his last prayer before setting out on the great voyage. Founded in the 15th-century, the church was largely rebuilt in the late 18th century.

Also in Calle Real, **Casa de Colón** (Columbus House) has no proven link with the explorer, but is now claimed as the house where he lodged. It has been restored as a museum about Columbus, featuring models of his ships and old maps, and is the focal point of the town's annual week-long Columbus festival in September.

Finally, in the harbourside park, the Torre del Conde (Count's Tower), is the oldest building in continuous use in the Canary Islands. This sturdy tower house dates from 1447, and was once the residence of Beatriz de Bobadilla, wife of the count of La Gomera, Hernán Peraza (whose father had built the tower). Both the count and the countess were hated by the Guanches for their repressive arrogance and cruelty. Hernán was eventually murdered for raping (or seducing) a Guanche princess, and Beatriz moved into this tower for her own protection.

The tower also has a connection with Columbus: after the murder of the count, Columbus became friendly with Beatriz. Later the tower became a storehouse for gold, silver and treasures looted from Native Americans and sent back to Spain.

✚ *La Gomera 4d* ✉ On the east coast of island 🍴 Bars in town (€); good food at the Parador de la Gomera (➤ 61) 🚌 The intermittent bus service is not reliable. Taxis are readily available at the ferry dock ❓ Fiestas include the local saint's festival around 20 Jan; Carnaval (Carnival) about the end of Feb (➤ 64–65); Semana Colombina (Columbus Week) 1–6 Sep; Virgen de Guadaloupe 1–6 Oct. Market open am daily except Sun for Gomeran craftwork and local products

🛈 Calle Real 4
☎ 922 141512

Pozo de la Aguada
✉ Calle Real ☎ 922 141512 🕐 Mon–Sat 9–1:30, 3:30–6, Sun 10–1 🎫 Free ❓ In the same building as tourist office

Iglesia Nuestra Señora de la Asunción
✉ Calle Real 🎫 Free

Casa de Colón
✉ Calle Real 56 ☎ 922 870155 🕐 Mon–Fri 10–1, 3:30–5:30, Sat 9–1 🎫 Free

VALLE GRAN REY

On the west side of the island is the majestic and remote Valley of the Great King, almost unknown until the 1970s, when it became something of a hippy retreat offering an away-from-it-all, ecologically sustainable lifestyle. Today, though, in spite of the location, it attracts more visitors than anywhere else on the island.

On the twisting road up to Arure (10km/6 miles inland), several viewpoints offer stunning panoramas of the cultivated terraces clinging to the lower slopes of the steep ravine, the scattered white houses and the valley opening out beside the vibrant blue sea. One hamlet has a spectacularly located *mirador* restaurant designed by Lanzarote architect César Manrique. The road descends to reach La Calera, the valley's attractive central community, amid banana plantations. Beyond, the road divides en route to the sea: to the north is La Playa; to the south the harbour at Vueltas, the traditional gateway to the valley. Both places have simple waterside eateries offering the freshest fish, and both have developed as tourist centres since the 1980s, their little shingle beaches among the best that La Gomera offers.

✚ *La Gomera 1d* ✉ 44km (27 miles) from San Sebastián 🍴 Many on the coast 🚌 Occasional buses and boats from San Sebastián
ℹ Calle Lepanto, La Playa, Valle Gran Rey ☎ 922 805458

VALLEHERMOSO

An attractive and appealing village – one of the island's largest
communities – Vallehermoso is indeed in a 'beautiful valley' as
its name suggests. It is surrounded by forest, vineyards and palm
plantations of date and banana. A striking 650m-high (2,132ft)
volcanic pinnacle close by is called Roque Cano, Dog Rock,
supposedly for its resemblance to a canine tooth.

✚ *La Gomera 2c* ✉ 48km (30 miles) northwest of San Sebastián

🍴 Bar-restaurants in the village centre (€)

HOTELS

HERMIGUA
Ibo Alfaro (€)
A delightful rural hostelry above the valley. The 19th-century building has been renovated in traditional style.
✉ Hermigua ☎ 922 880168; www.gomera-travel.com

PLAYA DE SANTIAGO
Jardín Tecina (€€€)
This impressive clifftop hotel, with magnificent gardens, has a beautiful pool and stirring views over the strait to Tenerife. 'Rooms' are in garden cottages.
✉ Lomada de Tecina ☎ 922 222140; www.jardin-tecina.com

SAN SEBASTIÁN
Parador de San Sebastián de la Gomera (€€€)
High above the port is this convincing copy of an early colonial mansion, furnished in Castilian style. Subtropical clifftop gardens command views over the town and coast.
✉ Llano de la Horca 1 ☎ 922 871100; www.parador.es

VALLEHERMOSO
Hotel Tamahuche (€)
This handsome former 19th-century manor house is now a simple but elegant, unpretentious and ecologically minded hotel.
✉ Calle Hoya 20 ☎ 922 801176; www.hoteltamahuche.com

RESTAURANTS

HERMIGUA EL TABAIBAL
El Silbo (€€)
Modest bar-restaurant just north of the village. Its flower-decked terrace is a lovely spot for a drink or meal with a view.
✉ Carretera General 102 ☎ 922 880304 🕐 Tue–Sun lunch, dinner

LAS ROSAS
Las Rosas (€)
This pretty roadside restaurant is an essential stopover on a tour of

La Gomera, for its demonstrations of *el silbo*, the island's unique whistling language. The Canarian specialities are very tasty, too.

✉ Carretera General, Agulo ☎ 922 800916 🕐 Lunch

SAN SEBASTIÁN
Casa del Mar (€€)

The seafood, notably the fish stew, at this nautical-theme restaurant has quite a following, among locals and visitors alike.

✉ Avenida Fred Olsen 2 ☎ 922 871219 🕐 Mon–Sat lunch, dinner; closed Sun

Parador de la Gomera (€€–€€€)

See page 61.

VALLE GRAN REY
Mirador César Manrique (€€–€€€)

Good food and fantastic views through wall-high windows at this remarkably located roadside restaurant.

✉ Carretera General, La Playa Calera ☎ 922 805868
🕐 Tue–Sun 12:30–8:45

SHOPPING

HANDICRAFTS AND SOUVENIRS
El Cercado

This village is famous for making traditional pottery (without the use of a potter's wheel) from the island's striking dark red clay, and many of the simple cottages here are pottery workshops.

Parque Nacional de Garajonay Visitor Centre

Good place for authentic, high-quality handicrafts – woodwork, banana-leaf baskets and musical instruments. See also page 69.

✉ Juego de Bolas, near Agulo ☎ 922 800993 🕐 Daily 9:30–4:30

ENTERTAINMENT/SPORT

La Gomera has almost no organized entertainment, sport or nightlife. Some hotels do put on low-key shows, and there are small discos.

Sight Locator Index

This index relates to the maps on the covers. We have given map references to the main sights of interest in the book. Grid references in italics indicate sights featured on the town plans and La Gomera island. Some sights within towns may not be plotted on the maps.

Index

189

Acknowledgements

The Automobile Association would like to thank the following photographers, companies and picture libraries for their assistance in the preparation of this book. Abbreviations for the picture credits are as follows – (t) top; (b) bottom; (c) centre; (l) left; (r) right; (AA) AA World Travel Library.

4l Puerto de Santiago, AA/C Sawyer; **4c** Mount Teide, AA/JTims; **4r** Barranco del Infierno, AA/J Tims; **5l** La Gomera, AA/C Sawyer; **5r** Jardines Marquesado de la Quinta Roja, AA/C Jones; **6/7** Puerto de Santiago, AA/C Sawyer; **8/9** Café in Playa de las Américas, AA/C Sawyer; **10/11t** Santa Cruz, AA/R Moore; **10c** Tile in Santa Cruz, AA/J Tims; **10bl** Garachico, AA/C Sawyer; **10br** Cats, AA/C Jones; **11c** Musician at Fiesta in Santa Cruz, AA/R Moore; **11b** Pico del Teide, AA/C Sawyer; **12/13t** People at restaurant, AA/C Sawyer; **12bl** Platter of fish, AA/J Tims; **12/13b** Mercado Nuestra Señora de África, AA/C Jones; **13tr** Paella, AA/P Bennett; **13c** Orange juice, AA/P Bennett; **14tl** Banana cheesecake, AA/C Jones; **14cl** Peppers at Mercado Nuestra Señora de África, AA/C Jones; **14/5** Farm worker, AA/C Sawyer; **15cr** Banana split, AA/C Jones; **15br** Banana liqueur, AA/C Jones; **16bl** Santa Cruz de Tenerife, AA/J Tims; **16br** Flower at Casa de Carta, AA/C Jones; **17** Pico del Teide, AA/C Jones; **18tl** Bananana Jardines de Atlántico, AA/R Moore; **18bl** Traditional dish, AA/P Bennett; **18/9** Arico, AA/C Jones; **20/1** Mount Teide, AA/JTims; **24** Fiesta Romera, AA/R Moore; **27** Ferry, AA/C Jones; **28/9** Santa Cruz Port, AA/C Jones; **30** Telephone, AA/C Sawyer; **31** Sign, AA/J Tims; **32** Policeman, AA/J Tims; **34/5** Barranco del Infierno, AA/J Tims; **36** Lace maker at Casa de los Balcones, AA/C Jones; **37** Casa de los Balcones AA/C Jones; **38/9** Drago Milenario tree, AA/C Jones; **40/1t** Caldera de las Cañadas, AA/R Moore; **40/1b** Cable car at Pico del Teide, AA/C Jones; **42/3** Garachico, AA/C Jones; **43t** Crest at Castillo de San Miguel, AA/C Jones; **44** Show at Loro Parque, AA/C Sawyer; **44/5** Loro Parque, AA/C Sawyer; **45** Alligator at Loro Parque AA/C Jones; **46** Los Gigantes, AA/R Moore; **47** Puerto de Santiago, AA/C Sawyer; **48/9** Mercado Nuestra Señora de África, AA/C Jones; **50** Casa de Carta, AA/J Tims; **50/1** Casa de Carta, AA/C Jones; **52t** Nuestra Señora de La Concepción, AA/R Moore; **52b** Nuestra Señora de La Concepción, AA/R Moore; **53** Nuestra Señora de La Concepción, AA/C Sawyer; **54/5** Pirámides de Güimar, AA/C Jones; **54** Pirámides de Güimar, AA/C Jones; **55** Pirámides de Güimar, AA/C Jones; **56/7** La Gomera, AA/C Sawyer; **59** Playa de las Teresitas, AA/C Jones; **60/1** Restaurant in Playa de las Américas, AA/C Sawyer; **62/3** Fountain, Jardines Marquesado de la Quinta Roja, AA/C Jones; **64** Fiesta Romera, AA/R Moore; **67** Marina at Puerto Colon, AA/C Jones; **69** Los Cristianos, AA/J Tims; **70/1** Aqua park, Playa de la Américas, AA/C Sawyer; **72/3** Pico del Teide, AA/C Jones; **74/5** Iglesia de San Juan Church, AA/C Jones; **77** Leather goods for sale, AA/R Moore; **78** La Gomera, AA/C Sawyer; **81** Restaurant in Playa de las Américas, AA/C Sawyer; **82/3** Jardines Marquesado de la Quinta Roja, AA/C Jones; **85** Parque Municipal García Sanabria, AA/C Jones; **86/7** Iglesia de Nuestra Señora de la Concepción, AA/C Jones; **88** Museo Militar Regional de Canarias, AA/R Moore; **88/9** Museo Municipal de Bellas Artes, AA/J Tims; **90/1** Parque Maritimo, AA/J Tims; **92** Parque Municipal García Sanabria, AA/C Jones; **93** Plaza de la Candelaria, AA/C Jones; **95t** Detail of ceramic bench, AA/C Jones; **94/5** Plaza de la Iglesia, AA/C Jones; **97** Cathedral at La Laguna, AA/C Jones; **98** Museo de la Ciencia y el Cosmos, AA/C Jones; **98/9** Museo de Historia de Tenerife, AA/C Sawyer; **100** Plaza del Adelantado, AA/C Jones; **101** Basilica de Nuestra Señora de Candelaria, AA/C Sawyer; **102/3** View of countryside from Casa del Vino La Baranda, AA/J Tims; **103** El Sauzal, AA/J Tims; **104** Basilica de Nuestra Señora de la Candelaria, AA/R Moore; **104/5** Town Hall, El Sauzal, AA/J A Tims; **106/7** Pirámides de Güimar, AA/C Jones; **107** Punta del Hidalgo, AA/C Jones; **108/9** Anaga foothills, AA/C Sawyer; **110** Cave dwellings, Anaga Peninsula, AA/C Jones; **110/11** San Andres, AA/C Jones; **119** Puerto de la Cruz, AA/C Sawyer; **120** Banana liqueur, AA/C Jones; **121** Banana flower at Bananera el Guanche, AA/C Jones; **122** Castillo de San Felipe, AA/C Jones; **123** Ermita de San Telmo, AA/C Sawyer; **124/5** Jardin Botánico, AA/C Sawyer; **125** Jardin Botánico, AA/C Sawyer; **127** Museo Arqueológico, AA/C Jones; **128** Plaza del Charco, AA/C Jones; **128/9** Bateria de Santa Barbara, © Eric James/Alamy; **130/1** Puerto de la Cruz, AA/C Jones; **132/3** Dragon tree at Icod de los Vinos, AA/C Sawyer; **133** Shop at Casa del Drago, AA/J Tims; **134/5** La Orotava, AA/C Jones; **135** Marquesado de la Quinto Rojo, AA/C Jones; **136** Fishing Boat, AA/C Jones; **137** Calle San Juan Street AA/C Jones; **138/9** Parque Nacional del Teide, AA/C Jones; **139** Cable car at Pico del Teide, AA/C Jones; **140** Las Cañadas, AA/C Jones; **151** Playa de las Américas, AA/C Sawyer; **152** Aqua Park, AA/C Sawyer; **152/3** Adeje, AA/J Tims; **154** Parque Ecológico Aguilas del Teide, AA/C Jones; **154/5** Playa de las Américas, AA/R Moore; **155c** Playa de las Américas, AA/R Moore; **156/7** Costa del Silencio, AA/J Tims; **157** El Médano, AA/J Tims; **158/9** Barranco del Infierno, AA/J A Tims; **160/1t** Vilaflor, AA/C Jones; **160/61b** Parques Exóticos, AA/R Moore; **162/3** Canary pines, AA/R Moore; **173** Terraces at Valle Gran Rey, AA/C Jones; **175** Hermigua, AA/C Sawyer; **176/7** Parque Nacional de Garajonay, AA/C Jones; **177** Playa de Santiago, AA/C Jones; **178/9** Parque Nacional de Garajonay, AA/C Jones; **180** San Sebastián de la Gomera, AA/C Jones; **182** San Sebastián de la Gomera, AA/C Jones; **184** Vallehermoso, AA/C Sawyer.

Every effort has been made to trace the copyright holders, and we apologise in advance for any accidental errors. We would be happy to apply the corrections in the following edition of this publication.

Dear Reader

Your comments, opinions and recommendations are very important to us. Please help us to improve our travel guides by taking a few minutes to complete this simple questionnaire.

You do not need a stamp (unless posted outside the UK). If you do not want to cut this page from your guide, then photocopy it or write your answers on a plain sheet of paper.

Send to: **The Editor, AA World Travel Guides,**
FREEPOST SCE 4598, Basingstoke RG21 4GY.

Your recommendations...

We always encourage readers' recommendations for restaurants, nightlife or shopping – if your recommendation is used in the next edition of the guide, we will send you a **FREE AA Guide** of your choice from this series. Please state below the establishment name, location and your reasons for recommending it.

_____
_____
_____
_____
_____
_____

Please send me **AA Guide** _____

About this guide...

Which title did you buy?
    AA _____
Where did you buy it?_____
When? <u>m m</u> / <u>y y</u>
Why did you choose this guide? _____
_____
_____
_____
_____

Did this guide meet your expectations?

Exceeded ☐   Met all ☐   Met most ☐   Fell below ☐

Were there any aspects of this guide that you particularly liked? _____
_____
_____
_____

continued on next page...

.Is there anything we could have done better? _____

_____

_____

_____

About you...

Name (*Mr/Mrs/Ms*) _____

Address _____

_____

_____ Postcode

Daytime tel nos _____

Email _____

Please only give us your mobile phone number or email if you wish to hear from us about other products and services from the AA and partners by text or mms, or email.

Which age group are you in?
Under 25 ☐   25–34 ☐   35–44 ☐   45–54 ☐   55–64 ☐   65+ ☐

How many trips do you make a year?
Less than one ☐   One ☐   Two ☐   Three or more ☐

Are you an AA member? Yes ☐   No ☐

About your trip...

When did you book? m m / y y   When did you travel? m m / y y

How long did you stay? _____

Was it for business or leisure? _____

Did you buy any other travel guides for your trip?

If yes, which ones? _____

_____

_____

Thank you for taking the time to complete this questionnaire. Please send it to us as soon as possible, and remember, you do not need a stamp (*unless posted outside the UK*).

AA Travel Insurance call 0800 072 4168 or visit www.theAA.com

---